JOURNEY

TO YOUR

KINGDOM DESTINY

*People who are destined to live
extraordinary lives!*

REX BURGHER

JOURNEY TO YOUR KINGDOM DESTINY

ISBN number: 978-1-935765-11-0

Requests for information should be addressed to:
Rex Burgher
Kingdom Life Ministry
P O Box 583
Dillsburg, PA
USA 17019

Phone: 717-502-0343
E-mail: info@klifemin.org
Web site: http://www.klifemin.org

1st Edition

DEDICATION

I want to dedicate this book to my Father in Heaven, with gratitude for including the ministry of reconciliation in the gospel message. You have given new hope to those of us who feel we've missed your perfect plan and have to settle for a sub-par destiny.

To the Apostle Peter, I want to personally thank you for being faithful to the words spoken over your life by Jesus in Luke 22:32. *"And when you have turned back, strengthen your brothers."* Thank you for not giving up on your destiny, showing us how to embrace the restoration Jesus offers us all.

I dedicate this to the millions who have felt like they have missed the mark and have fallen short of the plan God had prepared for them. May this book inspire you to rise up and reclaim your purpose and destiny.

I want to thank my wife, Lois for being my strength as I lived out the truths set forth in this book. You inspire me and complete me. I thank God for you each day for you are my perfect partner, best friend, and the sweetest love anyone could ever know. I am blessed and grateful that God put you in my life.

ENDORSEMENTS

In his book, *Journey to Your Kingdom Destiny*, Rex Burgher, has penned the very thing that the Holy Spirit seems to be saying to the church all across our nation: Deny yourself, take up your cross and follow Jesus. I believe that fulfilling our destinies is one of the ultimate goals of salvation- it's not just about "the sweet by and by!" In the book Rex teaches us that this lifelong journey is the under taught, second half of the Gospel wherein we are called, as Paul said, to work out our salvation with fear and trembling. The understanding of this theme is not a fad but one that is crucial to real discipleship and the maturation of the church. Read it. Absorb it. Live it.

Ben Scofield
Computer Software

Journey to Your Kingdom Destiny is an excellent book for those who want to fulfill their potential in life. Rex Burgher shares why many people get lost in their calling and then lays out a very practical guide of how one can get back on the right path in their God-given destiny. The very core of this book is the heart of the Father to see his kids restored and reconciled to him. Through this book you will read and gain insights of Biblical characters like Peter and David who fell and were restored to their destiny. I am very appreciative of Rex's grounding in Scripture and his practical tools in Part 2 of making conscious decisions to become your best you. This is a book that will healthily challenge your way of thinking about yourself and has the potential to powerfully impact your life if you choose to apply the Biblical principles Rex gives through this timely book. I highly recommend this to all leaders who help disciple or pastor individuals to see believers restored in their God-given destiny and new identity in Christ. Whether you have lost track in the past, are off your track now, or you are on the right track and want to see others come into their destiny then this is a book you want to read!

Timothy Berry
Founder of Hearts Ignited Ministries International
www.HIMinternational.org

In his latest book, <u>Journey to Your Kingdom Destiny</u>, Rex follows the transformation of the Apostle Peter's life from being ruled by the Kingdom of Self to total surrender to the Kingdom of God. We see our lives mirrored in these pages, the depth of Peter's love for Jesus, how his human impulsiveness and zeal for Christ in his own strength led him to a place of darkness, and of

Christ's redeeming love which teaches Peter how to walk in maturity and the fullness of his destiny. Peter's wisdom gives us "mile markers" for the journey of our lives, keys for walking in freedom and fruitfulness. I greatly appreciate Rex's open and transparent style, where his vulnerability to share his journey as well, inspires and gives us all courage to overcome our self-life and walk in Christ-likeness. This book is, to me, the reciprocal of Our Father's Heartbeat, where man responds to and journeys to live daily in the heartbeat of God.

Linda Forster
Founder of Covenant of Peace Ministries
www.covofpeace.org

"Journey to Your Kingdom Destiny" is a long awaited answer for generations of people who have questioned their God-given destiny and calling, and searched for a roadmap of how to achieve it. Rex Burgher provides a biblical blueprint that crosses all age, cultural, and social boundaries. Without giving a one-size-fits all "formula", Rex outlines a clear and simple process that anyone can relate to and immediately put into practice with confidence in their daily lives. We have heard many teachings on this topic, but none have been as concise and simply outlined as this. This book is an absolute must read!

Kevin and Dr. Amy Thompson DDS

The Father is calling, extending to us an invitation to walk in the tailor made destiny He has planned for His people. Rex Burgher helps cast vision and give the believer great expectations on the road to the fulfillment of God's calling in your life. Many have unanswered questions about the steps to take and what to expect on our journey forward. Rex boldly answers those questions and imparts courage to pursue the call in *Journey To Your Kingdom Destiny*.

Jamie Galloway
Director, Jamie Galloway Ministries
Sr. Pastor, East Gate Church
Author, *Supernatural Revolution*

My friend Rex, has been laying foundations for over 30 years first as a concrete contractor and now as a minister of the gospel. He has a keen eye to see with deep insight the work Christ is laying in you. I invite you if you are hungry for more of God, stuck in a rut and can't find your way out or simply disillusioned with the church, to partake in this journey to your Kingdom destiny.

Brandon Sundberg
Italian Plaster, Drywall Contractor

TABLE OF CONTENTS

PART 1

THE
JOURNEY
BEGINS

INTRODUCTION

*For ordinary people who are destined to live
extraordinary lives!*

Each one of us is born with a God-ordained destiny, a carefully drawn out plan for our lives. Before the beginning of time God knew us and put in motion a supernatural plan for our lives. It is important that we understand how significant each life really is to God. The plan for our life is so unique that the place in which we were born, the era in which we live, even the profession we currently have are especially suited for the fulfillment of that destiny. We are so special that no one who has come before us or who will come after us could do the very things he has created us to accomplish. God has chosen the circumstances that make up our life because, if followed, they give us the shortest route in reaching our destiny.

There are so many men and women that I have met who feel the mistakes they have made or the unfair consequences of what others have done have somehow negated them from reaching the destiny and purpose that God originally intended for their lives. Because of what happened in the past, they feel they must now settle for second best and live with the disappointments that come with living a life of "what-ifs".

What if I had never said those things?
What if I never made that mistake?
What if I hadn't crossed that line?
What if I still had that job?
What if that relationship hadn't ended?
What if I hadn't allowed myself to be falsely accused?
What if...

The roadmap we need to *keep* us on course or get us *back* on course is still available to us. If we do not realize that the journey to our destiny contains all of the successes and failures that we experience in life, we can easily find ourselves wandering aimlessly through life, constantly overwhelmed by a false sense of destiny—a destiny that makes us a slave to the circumstances of life. When that happens, we lose the strength to persevere so that we can stand victorious on the other side. There is someone who has not only gone on before us but who Jesus commissioned to help guide us through our times of testing. Luke 22:32, *"And when you* (speaking of Peter) *have turned back* (from your time of testing), *strengthen your brothers."*

Perhaps that is why Peter's life resonates so deeply within us, because in Peter we see ourselves. It is hard for us to find anyone in the Bible who has come to represent the universal man like

Peter. When we look at the good, the bad, and the ugly in Peter's life and what Jesus through the Holy Spirit made Peter into, each of us finds the hope that we also may run the race set before us and cross the finish line to hear the words of Jesus, "Well done, good and faithful servant." Peter's life has come to reflect the transformative work of God, which can bring restoration and hope to the lives of every believer no matter what has happened in our lives.

CHAPTER 1

AN ORDINARY LIFE

A destiny fulfilled and a life well lived.

Each of us has a destiny to fulfill, a purpose for being here. Whether we achieve or fall short of the goal that is before us rests solely on us. Situations do not control us, but how we handle those situations determines the outcome. Our success is not determined by whether or not we win, but how we influence the people and situations that God has placed before us for good and not evil.

We could be destined to live a simple life, never attaining the nobility that others aspire to or the fame with which some have been graced. Our life may consist of doing the simple things of life. And in doing those simple things, we may influence history just by being obedient to what He has so graciously placed within us.

Every wrinkle and line in our face tells a story and every gray hair a tale that turns each of us into a living portrait, one that conveys to those around us a glimpse into our lives. The outward picture is incomplete if it does not also show the circumstances that created the character that is now so much a part of who we are. The world has shaped us, circumstances have molded us, past failures and successes have defined us, and in the midst of it all we are mindful of what could have been. Every victory and defeat has etched a depth of character that is visible to the master. If you look closer, it will take you beyond death into that immeasurable place where time is no more.

The writers of the scriptures are no exception. Their lives are a portrait and their writings are an intimate look into their lives. Their life experiences gave them a depth of character that conveys the message of their hearts. Their letters are the canvas upon which all their messages are painted--and each writer has his own canvas, unique to himself.

For Peter, his story unfolds on the day Jesus passed by his boat and called him to be a fisherman of men; and Peter's remarkable decision to leave everything to follow him. I'm sure the people around Peter could hear the excitement in his voice when Peter spoke of the times on the Mount of Transfiguration when Moses and Elijah appeared. The telling of such stories would take Peter back in time as if once again he was on that mountaintop. I'm sure there were the times when, if you looked closely, you would see a fleeting smile come upon Peter's lips as he spoke of walking on the water with Jesus. Then there were the times when his voice became soft and tears would form at the corners of his eyes. In those moments, words failed, and Peter's voice faded as he became lost in a memory of his time with Jesus.

The life of Peter is the story of a man's personal destiny and his journey to fulfill that destiny. As we look at Peter's life story we will see that of our own journey to our personal destiny. Like Peter, everything we say and do reflects the hopes and dreams, disappointments and regrets we have experienced in our journey toward that destiny. That is why Peter gives us such hope and comfort. The insights into Peter's life have become for many of us a beacon that not only guides us in the dark times, but also keeps us focused on our journey toward the fulfillment of our personal destiny.

Peter's life is a story of transition from a Peter-centered life to a Christ-centered life. If we look closely, we can see how that transition affected Peter and the church. Peter's journey into his destiny and purpose is really the tale of two kingdoms: the kingdom of self and the kingdom of God. Both of these kingdoms are found within us and that is where the conflict begins. Each of us struggles and fights an internal civil war over who is in charge: "Is it I?" or "Is it God?" I fear the answer is, "It is I!"

Jesus said, *"If any man will come after me, let him <u>deny himself</u>, and <u>take up his cross</u>, and <u>follow me</u>."* Peter was willing to come but he had to first deny himself, take up his cross and follow Jesus. The first one seemed simple enough, the second almost destroyed him and the third became his life's story--the story of a destiny fulfilled and a life well lived. Peter's life story is our story as well and what he came through is the *rock* on which the church is built.

Peter made it through one of the most devastating experiences an individual can experience. When confronted in the garden, he denied that he ever knew Jesus. It is always one or the other--either you will deny yourself or you will deny Christ. Peter chose to deny Jesus and with that denial he saw himself for the person he actually was all along. Gone was all the bravado and the heroics and Peter was left with only his "self"--and what he saw almost destroyed him. Thank God that Jesus introduced the ministry of reconciliation into the church and restored Peter.

Peter never forgot what he had gone through or what his life would have been like if Jesus had not restored him. Now standing victorious on the other side, he never forgot the words that Jesus spoke over him: *"And when you have turned back, strengthen your brothers"* (Luke 22:31). Peter now stands on the other side, pointing out to us the path he walked and the lessons he learned, letting us know that what happened to him does not need to happen to us. But if it has, if you have felt like you have failed and fallen short, Peter words will encourage you to rise up! Your destiny still awaits!

As we progress on our journey and fulfill the destiny God has planned for us, we see ourselves change into the image of our Father in heaven. Because of our transformation into godliness, we do not respond as our old-nature previously dictated but take on a new nature, which bears the image of our Father in heaven. Godliness is that place of profound change in which you find the character of Christ manifested in your life. What does this new image look like? An image ruled by humility and purity of motives.

In the gospel accounts, Peter was a very earnest and devoted disciple of Jesus but on the inside there was still much of the old nature of Peter that still remained. In order for us to understand how Peter became the Peter of Pentecost and the writer of the Epistles, we must look back at his life and look at the self-willed, self-pleasing, self-relying, self-deceived, carnal Peter. Maybe then we will be able understand that what was in Peter may be in us as well.

If we were to do a survey to find out what person in the Bible (other than Jesus) most Christians identify with, the answer would often be the apostle Peter. No matter what it was about Peter that drew you to him, he is an incredible individual to study. As we look at his life, the trials he went through, the battles he won and lost, we will gain a perspective of our journey and discover the key to unlocking our own destiny and purpose.

Peter did have character flaws, but who doesn't? If you read the Gospel accounts, you can see that Peter was seemingly doing great. He made some mistakes, but what an incredible time it must have been. He was part of the twelve but even more so he was part of the inner circle closest to Jesus. When you are a part of the inner circle, you find special privileges that no one else has. Think of it for a moment. When people cannot get close to Jesus, everyone comes to you knowing that you have the master's ear. Especially when key, popular people come to you, it is natural to think of yourself as being of more importance than you should. You can really begin to think that you are something special not because of who you are as a person but because of your position--and that is a dangerous position to find yourself in. When your position becomes your identity, you excuse away any character flaws as being non-issues because your position points to the illusion that you are so much more.

What changed Peter from being the character we find in the gospels to the humble Peter we find later? Let's look at the man behind the image and find out why Peter has come to personify the common person.

CHAPTER 2

DEFINING PETER

What is in Peter is in us as well

L et us look at four stories found in the gospels that define the character of Peter. Peter was one of those chosen and, as we will see from these attributes of Peter, he was a good choice. He was not perfect by any means, but Peter would have been a quality pick for any church board. In fact, many of the attributes that Peter had are ones that we possess as well.

Many of us fall into one of three categories:

1. We have already experienced major disappointments in our lives, and because of the severity of the disappointment have never fully recovered from the mental, emotional and spiritual ramifications of that time in our lives.

2. We feel that we made it through the trial, a little damaged perhaps, but we worked through our disappointments.

3. We have not experienced anything like that in our life. In fact, our life is going along just fine and nothing has ever happened that we have not been able to process in a healthy way whether mentally, emotionally or spiritually.

Number three is how Peter's life was going. He was a successful businessman, hand-picked by Jesus, considered one of the three closest friends to Jesus, and a possible candidate to sit at the right or left hand of Jesus when the kingdom of God comes. I think we all would agree that he could be the poster boy for the successful and well-lived life. So let's take a look at the decisions that Peter made.

ENTIRE SURRENDER

Peter was a man of entire surrender to God and gave up everything to follow Jesus. Matthew 4:18-20 says, *"As Jesus was walking beside the Sea of Galilee, he saw two brothers, Simon called Peter and his brother Andrew. They were casting a net into the lake, for they were fishermen. 'Come, follow me,' Jesus said, 'and I will make you fishers of men.' At once they left their nets and followed him."*

I think this is an amazing story and speaks directly to the kind of person Peter was. Jesus is walking by the Sea of Galilee and sees two brothers Simon and Andrew. They are casting a net into the water and Jesus tells them to drop their net, forget their fishing business, and come with him because he would make them "fishers of men". To just drop your nets, put your boat in dry dock, and follow someone who just happens to be walking by and tells you to do so is inconceivable. Peter was impulsive and when he was behind something, he gave it 110%. Peter heard, believed, and surrendered everything to follow Jesus.

You may be saying to yourself right now that you would have done the exact same thing if Jesus had walked by you and asked you to "Come, follow me." When we think about it, he did ask us to "follow him", and we did--maybe not to the degree of giving up our business, but then we were never really asked to do that. When I was a young man there were a lot of "Jesus Freaks" around, usually young hippies who gave their hearts to Jesus and now were telling everyone they met about this Jesus. When I got saved, my unsaved friends would ask me if I was going to Africa yet. It did make me wonder if getting too close to Jesus would result in me being sent into the darkest jungles of Africa.

TRUE OBEDIENCE

Simon was also a man of true obedience. In another scriptural account, Simon had been fishing all night and caught nothing. He returned to shore empty but had to get ready for the next day so he began to clean his nets. After a while, a crowd began to gather around Jesus who was standing on the shoreline.

As Jesus was speaking to the crowd, he noticed two boats nearby and decided to get into one of them. The boat belonged to Simon and he had him push off from the shore a short distance. As they pulled back from the shore, Jesus sat down in the boat and began to teach the people. When Jesus had finished speaking, he said to Simon in Luke 5:4-5, *"Put out into deep water, and let down the nets for a catch. Simon answered, Master, we have worked hard all night and haven't caught anything. But because you say so, I will let down the nets. When they had done so, they caught such a large number of fish that their nets began to break."*

Simon was an expert at fishing. He had just finished fishing in that spot and there weren't any fish there. Peter told Jesus there were no fish based on his experience, but that did not mean that he disbelieved what Jesus was telling him. Peter let his nets down into the water. What occurred next must have been amazing to behold. The nets became so full that they frantically signaled others to bring their boat over to help them and they filled both boats with the fish they caught. Peter was a man of obedience. He did not grumble or complain but because Jesus said it, he believed it.

The one part of the dialogue that Peter had with Jesus that I have wondered at is when Peter says, "Because you say so, I will let down the nets." Most of us may have said the same thing as Peter but I do not think we would have been as positive about it as Peter was. It would be natural for us to say the same thing but under our breath or in the back of our minds we would be murmuring and complaining. After all, if you fished all night long and caught nothing and were told to go out again and cast your nets over the side you would be a little more than pessimistic. But let's be positive like Peter and not assume we would be anything but excited at the opportunity.

GREAT FAITH

Peter was also a man of <u>great faith</u>. Late in the night as the disciples were crossing the lake they saw Jesus walking on the water. They weren't sure exactly who was out there and they cried out with fear. *"Jesus immediately said to them: "Take courage! It is I. Don't be afraid." "Lord, if it's you", Peter replied, "tell me to come to you on the water." "Come, he said." "Then Peter got down out of the boat, walked on the water and came toward Jesus," (Matthew 14:27-29).*

I do not know many who would have had the courage to attempt what Peter was going to do much less actually do it. At first, they thought they saw a ghost! It had to be a strange site-- you do not see a man walking across a lake every day. When Jesus heard them crying out in fear he immediately called out to them. Peter must have recognized that it was Jesus voice, but even so his reply is interesting. This is not the usual request a typical person would make. Something in Peter saw an unbelievable opportunity. How many of us would see this encounter with Christ as an opportunity and grasp the chance to walk on water? Not many of us would think to do so, but Peter is an unusual man and he jumped at the chance.

Another thing that speaks of the boldness of faith in Peter is he had to get down from the boat into the water. Most would think that the boat was so low that you could just step over the side and onto the water, but it was not like that. The boat was large, at least large enough that you would have to lower yourself down the side. It really took courage for Peter to consider it much less actually go ahead, lower himself down from the boat, and stand on water. I have always thought that if Peter could have put his foot on the water to test it to see if it could hold up his weight before he committed the other foot, that act would not have been very courageous. But if he had to let himself go as he went over the side so that he had to drop into the water, *that* would take some faith. Walk or swim, the choice was Peter's and he jumped at the chance because he was a man of great faith.

SPIRITUAL INSIGHT

Peter was a man with incredible <u>spiritual insight</u>. When Jesus asked his disciples, *"Who do you say I am?"* *Simon Peter answered, "You are the Christ, the Son of the living God."* *Jesus replied, "Blessed are you, Simon Son of Jonah, for this was not revealed to you by man, but by my Father in Heaven,"* (Matthew 16:15-17).

I wonder if Simon Peter was as surprised by his answer as everyone else seemed to be. From looking at his life up to this point, it does not seem like this was the typical answer that he would have given, but then the law of averages would say that every now and then, you would get one right and maybe this was Simon Peter's time.

I find it interesting that Matthew records Peter's name here in the story above not as Simon (as it is in some of the writings) nor as Peter, but as Simon Peter. Simon was the name that was associated with his old nature and Peter was the name associated with his new nature, so writing his name as "Simon Peter" would indicate that in this account Peter got the answer right. Of course, it could have gone either way. He could have answered as the old Simon and gotten it wrong, but he answered in his new nature as Peter and it made all the difference.

I think we all have said things that have surprised us from time to time. I must say I like it when I get the answer correct but there have been times when I answered someone and even I was amazed at the wisdom and grace in which I responded. I just knew that was not my typical response.

I watched one day as a man was being totally thrashed by another person over a disagreement. I knew a little of what was going on, but just enough that I wanted to keep my distance and not get involved. After the one man was through ranting and raving, the other man began to speak. The wisdom and grace in which he responded was amazing to watch. He did not berate or get angry but in a calm and peaceful manner he responded in love. I watched the first man's face go from beet red to a normal tone, and his stance went from angry and confrontational to passive. They talked further back and forth, but the anger was gone from the discussion. It was like the man had been disarmed. At the end they hugged and the man thanked him for helping him to understand what had happened. One responded out of his old sin nature and the other out of the new nature. That new nature that is available to all of us if we would but learn the secret that Peter was about to learn.

CHAPTER 3

THE ROCK

The Foundation of the Church

When Peter answered the question, "Who do you say I am?" out of his new nature, Jesus said in Matthew 16:18, *"And I tell you that you are Peter, and on this rock I will build my church, and the gates of Hades will not overcome it."*

I have heard different teachings concerning this part of the scriptures. One is that Peter is the rock on which the church is to be built. This point becomes clear when we consider that the very bones of the Apostle Peter are said to be buried under the Basilica in Rome. For this reason, Catholics consider Peter to be the first Pope of the Catholic Church.

Let us consider that Jesus' reply was an indication to us that it is the *manner in which Peter received* the revelation that was the "rock on which the church would be built", rather than the revelation itself. Peter received the revelation not from his old nature but from his new nature. When our old nature has been

31

fully given over to Jesus and in complete submission to him, we are then able to draw from the new nature and that releases our ability to receive directly from our Father in Heaven. What's exciting is that when we receive revelation directly from our Father in Heaven, he gives us the ability to use the "keys to the kingdom of heaven" because we are speaking the very will of our Father. Jesus said, *"I will give you the keys of the kingdom of heaven; whatever you bind on earth will be bound in heaven, and whatever you loose on earth will be loosed in heaven,"* (Matthew 16:19).

When our will is in submission to the will of our Father in heaven, the prayers we pray will then be the very things that are on the heart of our Father. <u>Our will, submitted to his will, contains the keys of the kingdom of heaven that releases supernatural power so that, "whatever we bind on earth will be bound in heaven, and whatever we loose on earth will be loosed in heaven."</u> The rock the church is to be built upon is our will freely presented as a gift and in complete submission to the will of the Father.

I would imagine that Peter was very excited that he had answered correctly, but I would think he would have been even more excited over what Jesus had said concerning him. It is quite an honor to have Jesus telling you that you are the rock upon which the church will be built and you are the one to receive the keys to the kingdom. I wonder if Peter or any of the disciples understood what Jesus was saying to them? There have been times when people have told me things and then asked me if I understood. I may have said yes, but in reality my head was going from side to side saying no.

This is a very important part of scripture because it deals with how we as Christians arrive at answers to the questions posed to us. Our answers come either from God or from out of our old carnal nature. That is what Jesus was trying to get Peter and the disciples to understand when he asked him *"Who do people say that I am?"* Jesus was pleased when Peter answered correctly and quickly pointed this out to Peter and the disciples that the manner in which he received his revelation was what he was looking for.

Then Jesus said, *"And I tell you that you are Peter, and on this rock I will build my church."* The rock the church would be built upon was the revelation of having a mind set on the things of God and not the things of man. Jesus was saying to Peter and the disciples that, when they receive revelation like Peter, it doesn't come from you or from your carnal nature but it comes from your new nature through the Holy Spirit. It is on "that rock" of revelation that I will build my church.

Jesus was really saying, "Peter when you speak like you just did you are saying what is on my Father's heart. And when you do that, you will find in those words the keys to the kingdom.

When you speak my Fathers words you will see that, *"whatever you bind on earth will be bound in heaven."* Peter, when you have the mind of God rather than having your mind centered on the things of this world then, *"Whatever you loose on earth will be loosed in heaven."* When you get a revelation that comes from the natural or carnal mind, it is not based on the things of God but rather on the things of man. The things of man come out of our sin nature and do not contain the nature of God nor do they contain the keys to the Kingdom.

What happened next is where most of us shake our heads at Peter--but it is a perfect example of what happens when the things of man take precedent over the things of God. Even though time has passed between these two instances, it is a perfect example of Peter listening to his own carnal mind and not listening to the mind of Christ.

The story unfolds when Jesus talks about going to Jerusalem and suffering at the hands of the authorities, an event that will culminate with his death and resurrection. *"Peter took him aside and began to rebuke him, "Never Lord!" he said. "This shall never happen to you!"* Listen to how Jesus responded to Peter's rebuke: *"Jesus turned and said to Peter, "Get behind me Satan! You are a stumbling block to me, you do not have in mind the things of God, but the things of man."* (Matthew 16:22-23).

What a contrast! First, Peter is praised for not having the

mind of man but the mind of the Father. Now, Peter is told he has the mind of Satan, not the mind of the Father. Nothing takes the heavenly air of praise out from under our wings like a strong rebuke from Jesus.

This is one of the classic places in scripture that we just shake our heads at Peter. Peter actually forbids Jesus to go to the cross and die! He rebukes him for stating the Father's destiny and purpose for his life here on earth. No one can deny that Peter was a very devoted disciple of Jesus, but there was so much still lacking in Peter. The old-self was still strong within Peter. Peter's heart was full of self-pleasure, self-reliance, self-absorption and self-deceit. At times, Peter trusted in himself and his own thoughts about divine things. Yet when he yielded to God, Peter received incredible insights.

Here we are two scriptures that illustrate what happens when we receive from the mind of man versus the mind of God:

"They came to Capernaum. When he was in the house, he asked them, 'What were you arguing about on the road?' But they kept quiet because on the way they had argued about who was the greatest," (Mark 9:33-34).

"An argument started among the disciples as to which of them would be the greatest," (Luke 9:46).

35

The carnal man was strong within each of the disciples and often surfaced and exposed the true intentions of their hearts.

There comes a time when each of us needs to be converted from the self-life to the Christ-life. Each of us must come out from that place of self-pleasing, self-trusting, self-seeking and like Peter be filled with the Spirit and the life of Jesus. The same Christ that led Peter to his personal Pentecost is here today working in the lives of each one of us, leading us to our very own personal Pentecost. Often the question is simply, do we have in mind the things of God or do we have in mind the things of men? It is always one of the two; you will either deny "self" or deny "Christ".

CHAPTER 4

THREE SIGNS ALONG THE WAY

To deny himself, take up his cross and follow me!

Peter was soon to learn the meaning of the sentence found in Matthew 16:24: *"If anyone would come after me, he must deny himself and take up his cross and follow me."* The journey that Peter was about to undertake was the most significant one of his life. If he lived through it, it would also be the most life changing. To come to the end of yourself will cost you everything.

There is not one person who has taken this journey who really understood the fullness of it until they lived through it and stood victorious on the other side. Our vision is always much clearer afterwards, once the fullness of the revelation is revealed. In Peter's story, we see a far different man standing on the other side of his personal Pentecost than we saw in the man who walked beside Jesus for three years. Gone was all the bravado and grand standing and we are left with a humble man, full of grace and mercy.

Like Peter, we probably do not understand the meaning of what it takes to follow Jesus. We often nod our heads as if we fully understand this statement when in reality we really have no concept of what it means at all. How can you understand something you have yet to experience? Even if I were to say to you that only when you come to the end of yourself will you really be able to find yourself--you may nod in mental agreement but the journey to the end of all our self-justifying, self-pleasing, self-edifying, self-worship will come at a hard cost to you.

The journey to the end of yourself will cost you everything. Not everyone is willing to take the journey nor does everyone make it through the journey to the destiny that God has planned for them. Jesus says over and over in the book of Revelation, "to him who overcomes" I will give the gift of eternal life. What is it that we must overcome? That cursed unredeemed self-life with all its petty excuses for remaining the same, never changing, and always struggling--that is what we must overcome. Why do so many men and women of God fail? It is because they have not come to the end of themselves.

As hard as it is for most of us to come to the end of ourselves, it is even harder for those who are famous or wealthy. Jesus said in Matthew 19:24, *"Again I tell you, it is easier for a camel to go through the eye of a needle than for a rich man to enter the kingdom of God."* Why is it so hard for those with fame or fortune? When life is easy--when you have money, prestige, given honor for your accomplishments, given the best seats, the most applause--then it becomes hard for you to consider that you have to deny yourself. Success can be a great test of character. Self-deception is so deceiving that the person who is self-deceived hardly notices the deception. All of us, rich or poor, fat or thin, famous or not, are called to come to the end of ourselves. This is the beginning of the journey into our destiny.

DENY HIMSELF

To really understand how to deny ourselves, we need to look at Luke 14:26 where Jesus tells us that we must hate our own life if we are to be his disciple. Jesus said, *"If anyone comes to me and does not hate...yes, even his own life...he cannot be my disciple."* The word translated "life" is "soul", which is the seat and center of the self-life with all of its self-serving attitudes, choices, and activities.

All of this began when Adam and Eve sinned in the garden. They believed that if they ate from the tree of the knowledge of good and evil they would *"be like God, knowing good and evil,"* (Genesis 3:5). Our sin nature is "self's" desire to be equal with God. Each individual born from that point onward has been born with the nature to self-rule.

Within the heart of each person born is a god-throne, a place reserved for God. But because of our rebellion, we have placed ourselves on the throne. The king that rules on our throne is our personal identification, our ego. Our ego or "self" is the king who sits on the throne and rules the kingdom within us. King self remains king until his kingdom begins to fall apart. It is at this point that the old king is in need of someone to save him from his predicament. It is not just anyone that can help because the king is prideful enough to only seek help from another king, preferably one of his stature that understands him.

The old king is looking for someone to save him from the embarrassment of his kingdom falling apart. It is at this time that the hold the old king has had over our heart begins to slip away and we hear Jesus knocking on the door of our heart calling us back home. But we seldom realize that this Savior comes as Lord and King, bringing with him a new and holy kingdom. This new King is holy and his kingdom is holy as well.

The old king stands off to the side and watches everything that the new King is doing. He may not approve of the changes, but he is too weak to stop anything from happening. So he waits and, like Absalom the son of King David, he returns dressed in religious robes. He sits at the gate and tells you that he has the ear of the King and if the new King seems far away and busy, he will always be available. Our free-will gives us the choice to choose whom we will listen to and, if the old king knows anything, he knows how to be crafty and deceptive.

The kingdom of God and the kingdom of self are within each believer. There is an internal civil war taking place in the heart of every believer until either the new heaven and new earth appear or until we pass from this earth. We can overcome the old king and live a victorious life, but we must always be vigilant or he will return and cause havoc in our lives.

Our will was once blameless, but because of our willful decision to eat from the tree of the knowledge of good and evil it has become subject to the forces of good or evil. For our will to remain free, it must make the right choices and not the wrong ones. The will has the power of control over one's own actions or emotions. The will has the authority or power to determine which goals are accomplished. The old saying, "As the will goes so goes the man," is very true.

The problem we face is our 'will" has been badly scarred from years of being abused by our sin-nature. Since we cannot trust in our ability to make quality decisions, we find it difficult to trust ourselves. Of course, that leaves us with only God to trust. At this point, we need our will to come into alignment with the will of the Father. It is the will which has the power to change us and give us the determination to see that we stay changed.

That is the central problem humanity faces with becoming a true disciple of Jesus. Peter was just ready to learn the first of these great lessons, but to do this he would have to see himself for who he truly was. You cannot come to the place in your life where you will honestly deny yourself until you come face to face with yourself. God knows how to bring us to that place where we see ourselves for what we are really like. And when we see what we are capable of doing, when every excuse is stripped away and we are faced with the realization that what is in me is just so much of my old nature, then I have no choice but to come to the end.

Our religious garments hide so much of who we really are, for we are so much like Peter--doing all the right things for all the wrong reasons. Pride has a way of rising up and taking credit for everything we do, even if it is done for honorable purposes. When Jesus says to deny yourself, it is in that place where our identity or our ego resides. It is in the place where we have allowed the old nature to have residence. We have the promise that when we accepted Jesus as our Savior and Lord, that he will come with a new kingdom that is found within us. The problem is we often furnish this new kingdom with all of the self-justifying, self-pleasing things that we had left over from our old kingdom.

Many of us, when we accepted Jesus as our Lord and Savior, really had given no thought to the fact that he comes as a package deal and we ignored the "Lord" part of the deal. We just wanted someone to save us out of our current condition, and that is why we cried out for a Savior. Once we got our lives back to normal, we would take back our right to rule and reign over our lives. The thought of coming to the end our "selves" probably had not occurred to you--it certainly did not occur to me. To do this I would have had to deny my "self" the right to rule and reign as my Lord and King. The truth is that not all of us have fully come to the end of self—at least not yet. But the writing is on the wall.

If you are wondering just how our fragmented "self" has become, let us look at the term *self-justification*. Self-justification occurs when a problem arises between you and someone else. If we are honest, we often view our part in the problem as being mostly honorable. That does not mean that we are blameless. I am sure if asked we would humbly admit that we did make some mistakes in how we handled things. This is often seen in either our apology or in our explanation of what happened when we talk to others. We begin by telling them what happened. We hold the high ground by letting everyone know that we had the best of intentions. We may even go so far as to admit that we did make mistakes but that you know my heart and I would never intentionally harm anyone.

I have to be justified to myself and everyone else that, even though what I did might have been wrong, what the other person did was even worse. Even on the rare occasions when I do confess to someone that I made some errors in judgment, I negate my excuse with the word "but", which is followed by a long list of the things the other person did to provoke me. The bigger your 'but" is the bigger the game of self-justification is within you. That is why we explain our actions as being considerate, but the actions of others as being inexcusable and highly suspicious.

A wealthy young man said to Jesus, *"Teacher, 'he declared', all these things I have kept since I was a boy."* (Mark 10:20-21). This young man wanted Jesus to know all the good he had done throughout his life. Jesus looked at him said, *"One thing you lack, he said, Go, sell everything you have and give to the poor, and you will have treasure in heaven. Then come, follow me."* There was one last stronghold in the life of the rich young man that he needed to overcome and that was his reliance on his finances. The hold these finances had over his life was summed up in verse 22, *"At this the man's face fell. He went away sad, because he had great wealth."* The truth was this, his possessions had him.

When we cut a person off in traffic or yell at someone who does not move fast enough when the light turns, we have to justify our actions to ourselves or face the realization that we are the ones with the problem and in need of change.

Jesus said to Peter and to each one of us that we should, "deny yourself" with all your self-pleasing, self-serving, self-justifying attitudes and pick up our cross.

TAKE UP HIS CROSS

The truth is that many of us do not like our cross. If you are like me, you think that everyone else has a better cross to bear than you do. Whether it is a world known evangelist or a popular book author or a pastor of a huge church or a successful businessman, their cross seems bright and shiny, but not our cross. Our cross looks old, decrepit, and full of splinters. Perhaps someone with a greater anointing, who is a gifted speaker--their cross would be a much nicer one to bear. My cross does not seem as appealing as everyone else's cross. Ours has splinters, knots, it is crooked and at time's we feel like kicking it with our foot as if to see if there is something hiding under it.

When Jesus mentions picking up our cross, he is describing the total sum of the life we live; it is who we are and are meant to be and it could be as varied as the cross Jesus carried, to any other cross in the history of mankind. <u>Whatever our cross is, whatever our lot in life is, we need to accept it, pick it up, and carry it.</u> Jesus is saying, get over yourself, pick up your cross your purpose for being here and come follow me. Deny yourself, with all the bickering and complaining concerning what you can or cannot do, and follow me. Do not worry about tomorrow for tomorrow has enough problems of its own. Stop thinking about yesterday for who can change what has already happened? Learn to live in the moment and enjoy life. You cannot pick up your cross successfully if you are doing it begrudgingly or with trepidation. Picking up your cross is done with the understanding that this cross was made just for you because it offers the shortest route to your destiny and purpose.

Peter says in 2 Peter 1:3, *"His divine power has given us everything we need for life and godliness through our knowledge of him who called us by his own glory and goodness."* It is true that many of us have not reached the point where we have overcome our sinful nature and have put to death the old man within. You can often find yourself trapped in cycles that hold you in bondage to your old king within. You go to a church until you run into a difficult situation with a group of people and so you to run to another church. After a few years, you find yourself faced with the same situation as you had previously found yourself in. Why is that? It is because God has a test for you and he will never let you fail the test because he always schedules a makeup test for you. You can go through life till you're seventy years old going from one make up test to another make up test as God patiently waits for you to come to the end of yourself. <u>Rather than pray for the mountain that looms before you to disappear, pray that you have the strength to go through the mountain of adversity and stand victorious on the other side.</u>

FOLLOW ME

The truth is that your cross is your life's roadmap to your destiny and purpose. Peter says in 1:4, *"He has given us his very great and precious promises, so that through them you may participate in the divine nature and escape the corruption in the world caused by evil desires."*

What was it about Peter that caused him to be so different after Jesus reinstated him? When you have come to the end of yourself, there is a settling within your spirit as to what life is about. Before you went wherever you wanted to go, you did and said pretty much what you thought you needed to say or do to arrive where you wanted to end up. Peter had dreams, and he was found arguing with the other disciples over who was the greatest in the kingdom.

Then there came a time when he saw himself for who he really was inside and it broke him. When you are broken like that, you do not trust the intentions of your heart. You become slower to speak and kinder of heart. After Jesus restored Peter, he said to him, *"Feed my sheep. I tell you the truth, when you were younger you dressed yourself and went where you wanted; but when you are old you will stretch out your hands, and someone else will dress you and lead you where you do not want to go,"* (John 21:17-18). Then he said to Peter, "Follow me!"

We must realize that where we live, what we do, or what era we live in does not matter as much as the *way* in which we live in the here and now. If we carelessly go about our daily lives with just the thought of preserving our lifestyle and getting a good wage, then what does that say about the motives that shape our character? <u>May God open our eyes to see that the lives we touch, touch the lives of others who in turn touch others in an ever-widening ripple throughout eternity.</u>

What if we were able to go about our life, day in and day out, year after year, with no thought of human notice? Everyone around would love a person who spent his life in the pursuit of making others happy. Each of us was chosen since the beginning of time to fulfill great and awesome tasks. It is true that life is found not in doing of great things, but in daily doing small things in a great way.

CHAPTER 5

PETER'S LIFE MESSAGE

We all have a story to tell!

Close to the end of his life and alone in his cell, Peter took pen in hand and began to write his life message. Let us look at II Peter 1:3. In the New International Version, they call this section, "Making One's Calling and Election Sure". Peter writes, *"His divine power,* (that is God's power), *has given us everything we need for life and godliness through our knowledge of him who called us by his own glory and goodness.* (His power in us has given us everything we need, we are lacking nothing to achieve the purpose and destiny he has for our lives.) *Through these, he has given us his very great and precious promises, so that through them you may participate in the divine nature* (that is becoming like God in all its purity and love, goodness and mercy) *and escape the corruption in the world caused by evil desires."* (the corruption of those evil desires, that is our old nature that wages war inside of us through our sin nature.)

"For this very reason, make every effort to add to your <u>faith</u>

49

goodness; and to <u>goodness</u>, knowledge; and to <u>knowledge</u>, self-control; and to <u>self-control</u>, perseverance; and to <u>perseverance</u>, godliness; and to <u>godliness</u>, brotherly kindness; and to <u>brotherly kindness</u>, <u>love</u>."

"For if you possess these qualities in increasing measure (that means it gets better and better and better) *they will keep you from being ineffective and unproductive in your knowledge of our Lord Jesus Christ.* (If we stop along the way and fail to completely give ourselves over in every area of our lives we run the danger of being unproductive in his plan for our lives.) *But if anyone does not have them, he is nearsighted and blind, and has forgotten he has been cleansed from his past sins."*

"Therefore, my brothers, be all the more eager to make your calling and election sure. For if you do these things, you will never fall, and you will receive a rich welcome into the eternal kingdom of our Lord and Savior Jesus Christ."

When I first read this scripture, one thing that struck me was the part of being ineffective and unproductive in our knowledge of the Lord. It was not something I wanted as a part of my life. The idea of "falling" does not sound appealing to me either. That is why these verses were highlighted in my spirit, because I did not want to be ignorant of what Peter was telling me.

As I studied these scriptures, I realized that in verses five through seven Peter was emphasizing eight sign posts that point out what every Christian needs to be aware of, especially if you wish to avoid the pitfalls of an ineffective and fruitless life. Each one of these complements the next and helps us to be productive in our knowledge of our Lord and Savior. Faith, goodness, knowledge, self-control, perseverance, godliness, brotherly kindness and love each build upon the other and help us grow from glory to glory.

Let's begin to look at the significance of how these complement each other. Let's look specifically at the last three that Peter mentions: godliness, brotherly kindness, and love. These three mirror the Great Commandment and the Great Commission. Oftentimes the church puts the Great Commission ahead of the Great Commandment. Let me explain. The Great Commission in Matthew 28:19 says, *"Therefore go and make disciples of all nations, baptizing them in the name of the Father and of the Son and of the Holy Spirit, and teaching them to obey everything I have commanded you."* In this verse Jesus is commissioning us to go out to the lost, proclaim the good news that the kingdom of God is at hand, baptize them, and make them disciples of Jesus Christ. As Christians, we are commissioned to do this and rightly so.

Let's look at the Great Commandment which is found in Matthew 22:37-39 which says, *"Love the Lord your God with all your heart and with all your soul and with all your mind. This is*

the first and greatest commandment. And the second is like it:
Love your neighbor as yourself."

If we put so much emphasis on the Great Commission that we put its importance ahead of the Great Commandment, then we could easily end up making disciples that look more like ourselves than the one we love with all our heart, soul and mind-- Jesus! In *Webster's Dictionary* a disciple is defined as *one who undertakes the disciplined instruction from another individual with the sole intent that we adhere to their teaching taking on their characteristics and life patterns.* That is why Jesus taught in the Rabbinical Method of teaching that was popular in his day. The Rabbinical Method required that the student had to come and live with the teacher so the student could not only listen to the teacher, but take on his mannerisms as well.

Often people can tell who influenced you by what you emphasize in your teaching and even in the way you present yourself to others. I can tell if a speaker sat under John Wimber by the laidback style of teaching, the clothes he or she wore, and the way that speaker sounded. Similarly, you can recognize those who sat under Chuck Smith of Calvary Chapel or Kenneth Hagin of the Word of Faith movement by the way they talk, their dress, and mannerisms. We pick up these styles because we tend to emulate the people we want to be around. Most of us pick up things by osmosis, by picking up things consciously and subconsciously. If the truth be known, it is probably more of the latter than the former.

Later on in the second letter written by Peter, the apostle warns us about false teachers. That is why it is so important that we listen to Peter and understand the points that he is making so we will become those who are true disciples of Jesus and thus raise up others who are true disciples as well. If we do not grab hold of these principles that Peter laid out for us, there is a very good chance that we will be deceived because we are nearsighted and blind.

Let's look at your parents. When someone reminds you that you are just like your father or mother, have you ever noticed it is hardly ever a good compliment? Usually they are referring to some habit or quirk they had that always irritated those around them. It is a strange twist that we often end up doing the very thing that our parents did that irritated us the most. In fact, we often pick up many little habits, such as the way we do and say things or how we react in a situation, more than we do the spoken words. The saying "Do as I say and not as I do," is one we would like our kids to listen to, but in reality they pick up far more by what we do than by the instructions we give them. Our actions are screaming while our mouths may be saying something very different. As someone once said, "You really need to tone down your body language. It is screaming so loudly that I cannot hear what your voice is saying."

Peter learned that if we do not put the heart of the Great

Commandment ahead of the Great Commission we could easily end up with disciples that look more like ourselves and very little like the Lord we serve and love. All of the eight points that Peter mentions build upon each other and help each one of us to put to death the old nature so we can take on the new nature becoming like our Lord and Savior in all that we do and say.

I do not think there are any of us out there that like eight steps to anything, especially when they contain words like self-control and perseverance, which sounds like a lot of work. Steps tire us out. It is like going on a diet. Who looks forward to dieting? In reality, we all are secretly longing to see a pill come on the market that enables us to eat all the pizza in the world and lose weight while doing it. So for the time being, let us skip over the steps and go to things that excite us.

Let's look at the words *calling* and *election*. These words excite us because they speak of destiny and purpose. We also need to understand what the word *calling* means. To many, just receiving a prophetic word is all they want. They do not want to go through the process that it often takes for the word to become a reality. Human nature says that if it is going to take work then I would rather wait for another prophetic word from another prophet that would take no suffering or commitment on my part for it to happen.

Look at Peter. He had one of the most powerful prophetic words spoken over him that a person could possibly have.

"Upon this rock I shall build by church.... and I will give you the keys." After that word, you could easily put your thumbs in your suspenders and strut around with definite feelings of grandeur. That was a very powerful word and the fact it was Jesus who said it, only added to its significance.

We know that the rock mentioned in the prophetic word was in reference to Peter and that he was the rock on which the church would be built. But few of us realize that before Peter could be the rock he would have to deny his "self" the right to rule and reign in his life and give his life over in total submission to Jesus, making Jesus his Lord. The rock upon which the church is built is centered on each one of us giving our lives over in total submission to Jesus as Lord and King over us. Then we can become the person we have been destined to become and also receive the keys to the kingdom. For Peter that meant he would have to fall in the outer courtyard when he denied Jesus and come to the end of himself. We can settle for second best and live a very good life in the kingdom, but if you want the fullness of your destiny and purpose that awaits you, then must go through the journey as Peter and so many others have done.

Peter left us a roadmap of that journey. In 2 Peter 1: 5-7, Peter points out some signs that we need to be aware of along the way. Let us take a few minutes and look at a couple of those signs, calling, and election that are crucial in our journey to our destiny.

CHAPTER 6

EVERY JOURNEY HAS A MAP

Landmarks along the way

According to *Webster's Dictionary*, a calling is *a profession, trade or occupation that you do.* In other words, it is what you are currently doing right now. Whether you are a schoolteacher, dentist, businessman, brick layer, student or lawyer your "calling" is what you are currently doing.

Peter also speaks of us having an election, which is defined by *Webster's Dictionary* as *the process of filling an opening.* Almost all elections involve deciding to fill an opening by following the necessary steps required by the person to achieve the position.

Even though we currently have a calling or a commitment on our daily lives based on what we are doing right now, there is an election out there for us to fill if we do the necessary steps to achieve our new position. When we successfully do the requirements necessary to move into the new place, it then becomes our "calling" and we stay there fulfilling the obligations that we have until another "election" comes before us. We go from calling to election until that election becomes our new calling followed by another election and on and on until we come to our place of destiny and purpose that God has for us.

FROM SHEPHERD TO KING

The Life of King David

King David's life is perhaps one of the best illustrations of the journey to your destiny. David experienced both callings and elections before he ever arrived at his destiny. The first mention of David in the Bible is when he was a young sheepherder to his father's sheep. If you remember, Samuel the Prophet was sent to David's village by God to anoint the next King over all of Israel. Samuel is one of the most prominent prophets mentioned in the Old Testament. Samuel is not like other prophets who come to churches to bless the people by bringing only words of encouragement to them.

When Samuel comes to town, we find everyone is not so excited about the prophet coming, and rightly so, because Samuel doesn't mess around as a prophet of God. When Samuel arrives in your town, you really are not too sure if he is going to prophesy something positive or negative to you. We find in the scriptures that it was not uncommon for the leaders of the towns and villages to go out to meet Samuel on the outskirts of their village. They were worried about what he might say, so they wanted to know if this was something that was either good or bad. In fact, in 1 Samuel 16:4, it says they *"trembled when they met him."*

How would it be if a prophet came to your church and, through the Holy Spirit, this prophet knew everything about you-- the good, bad, and ugly things about your life? What if this person had some God-given knowledge about your past sins and he said he was there to expose them to everyone? I have been in groups of people when prophets have come and when they do you can see everyone in the congregation sitting on the edge of their seats, hoping they will get called on. They want to receive a word from God and hear all the positive things that God has for them.

You can just see the excitement in their eyes, hoping the prophet will glance in their direction so they could somehow catch his eye and be noticed. What do you think would happen if he called on a few people and not only spoke of the positive, but also exposed their deep hidden sins! I can just see the people slide down in their seats and try to disappear. Where previously they tried to make eye contact, now they try not to be noticed. Such was the gifting of the prophet Samuel.

We see that when Samuel came to town it was serious

business, and this time was no exception because he was coming to anoint the next king over all of Israel. Samuel is more than a little nervous inside about what he has been sent to do. In fact, Samuel said to God in 1 Samuel 16:2, *"How can I go? Saul will hear about it and kill me."* Everyone knew that there was a king currently on the throne and it was not the brightest or healthiest thing to do to go and anoint a new king before the old one was gone. We see God gave Samuel a strategy and off he goes. In 1 Samuel 16:2-3 it says *"The Lord said, "Take a heifer with you and say, 'I have come to sacrifice to the Lord.' Invite Jesse to the sacrifice, and I will show you what to do. You are to anoint for me the one I indicate."* In this manner God gave Samuel a way in which he could go and anoint the new king without Saul finding out.

If we have learned one thing from Samuel's life, it is that he is completely obedient to God. So when God says "go", Samuel is already packing his bags. When Samuel arrived at the home of Jesse he has him bring all his sons before him and Samuel goes through each of the sons looking for the one that God will point out as the next King. For Samuel, the task was not an easy one, for each of the sons had attributes that the natural eye would find appealing in a king. However, as each one came forward it was obvious to Samuel that the Lord was not interested in them.

Finally the last son in the room left. Samuel asks of Jesse, *"Are these all the sons you have?"* Jesse answered, *"There is still the youngest, but he is tending the sheep."* Then Jesse sent for David so that Samuel could see him. When he came before Samuel God said, *"Rise and anoint him; he is the one."*

Samuel anointed David by pouring a "horn of oil "over his head. Now this is not your usual drop of oil that we typically see in churches. When Samuel anoints you with oil, you know you have been anointed because he pours a full horn of oil over David's head. It says in the word, *"And from that day on the Spirit of the Lord came upon David in power."* There was no one in the land that did not believe that Samuel's prophesies were from the Lord. And now that he anointed David, there was no doubt that what was proclaimed would come about.

DAVID THE SHEPHERD

I am sure David's mind was reeling from the prophetic words of destiny that Samuel had just spoken over him. However, David had a calling and right now all he could hear was the distant sound of, "Baaaaa, baaaaa, baaaaaa." It was the sheep and David's calling was... calling. So David returns to tend the sheep, even though he had just received a powerful revelation of what God had in store for him. Remember, Peter pointed out to us there is an election awaiting David which will guide and prepare him for his destiny.

I wanted to make an observation from my own life and

perhaps it will be applicable our understanding David's life.

It is natural for someone who receives a prophetic word to want to see it come to pass-- the more glamorous the word the sooner we want to see it. Most of us are not excited that there is often a process that must take place for the word to become a reality. If the process appears to require effort on our part then we would prefer to hear another word, perhaps this new word would not take any effort on our part for it to come true. We must wait for the opportunities that God has preordained so that the words come to pass in his timing and for his glory.

It says that after Samuel anointed David king, *"the Spirit of the Lord came upon David in power,"* (1 Samuel 16:13). Something must have been settled within David's heart for him to know that it was not his responsibility to make things happen, but it was his responsibility in how he reacted to the circumstances of life. Whatever it was that happened as he took care of the sheep, there was something about David that gave him the confidence that the circumstances of life were opportunities. David had a quiet assurance that nothing could stop him from becoming king. Perhaps that is what was going through his mind when he killed the lion and the bear and as he ran towards Goliath with such boldness and determination.

The election that was before David was becoming armor bearer to the King. Because of the faithfulness to his last calling,

David had fulfilled all the requirements of his former position. Now he was ready to assume his new position as armor bearer. As he steps into his new calling as armor bearer, he left behind his old calling as sheepherder. The journey toward his destiny is progressing.

DAVID THE HARPIST

Each one of us has a destiny, a God-ordained purpose to our lives. As we journey through life, the callings that come our way last for a season of time. The length of each season may be as different as the calling we may have to do. I am sure David's strength and skill in the killing of Goliath brought on the next election faster than anyone could imagine. Many of us probably would have thought that David's next election would be as a general or at least a high position in the land. After all, he just defeated Israel's greatest enemy. But that was not to be the case, and David was not discouraged about his new position as armor bearer. For David, the season as armor bearer to the king did not last long because there was another election out there. Next, he was elected to be the harpist for the King.

David is in the palace of the King and one could almost see the pattern that is evolving here as he begins the process of fulfilling his destiny. First, he was out tending the sheep. Then he became armor bearer for the King and now harpist to the king, which brought him inside the palace. David is moving up the corporate ladder of success and, in the natural, you can almost see how things are beginning to work out for David. In the corporate world, David is on the fast track for kingship.

Saul was tormented within his spirit and when David played the harp, the tormenting spirit would leave Saul. (See 1 Samuel 16:14). For most of us, it would seem like everything was working out well. David was finally eating good food and sleeping indoors for the first time in years. We would think it was an answer to our prayers, especially now that songs were coming to his mind, the anointing was flowing, and the evil spirit would depart from Saul.

It was in this setting that something happened that changed everything for David. But, for the moment, David was enjoying his life. The way things were working out, you could almost see David trying on crowns to see which one fit because everything seemed to be heading in the right direction.

David's life seemed to on the fast track to his destiny. The bad news was that there was a "new election" on the horizon and it was coming toward David faster and in a way that would surprise David.

"But an evil spirit from the Lord came upon Saul as he was sitting in his house his spear in his hand. While David was playing the harp, Saul tried to pin him to the wall with his spear,

but David eluded him as Saul drove the spear into the wall. That night David made good his escape," (I Samuel 19: 9-10).

David's "election" came fast and furious in the form of a javelin out of nowhere! The javelin barely missed David and almost pinned him to the wall. Who threw the javelin? The current king threw the javelin--he was obviously upset. Ever have one of those "suddenly" moments when you know that this is not going to turn out all that good? David's "suddenly" moment took him from climbing the corporate ladder of success to hiding for his life in the cave of despair.

DAVID THE CAVE DWELLER

Something does not seem to fit. David was doing so well. He was climbing the corporate ladder to the penthouse. All of a sudden, David finds himself in that place of being a cave dweller. This is the most important lesson we can learn on our journey to our destiny. <u>What appears to be demotion in the eyes of the world could very well be a promotion in God's eyes</u>. We need to start looking at things the way God looks at things instead of looking at them as the world looks upon life's situations. Deny yourself the luxury of having a negative attitude over all the grief and frustration that comes out of a bad situation. You can have a positive attitude if you look for the opportunities that the situation provides for you.

Can you imagine what it must have been like to be chased into a cave and then have to live in one? David found himself in an actual cave, but many of us have found ourselves feeling like we have been chased into the wilderness and the place we are at might as well be a cave. There are many reasons you may find yourself in a cave. You can self-justify it until you are blue in the face, but the fact of the matter is that you are in one and it is not pleasant. It is especially hard being in a cave when you feel you are falsely accused and the person who accused you will not let you alone. In fact, they are trying to destroy you!

What makes it even more difficult being a cave dweller are all the crazy people who begin to congregate in your cave. For some reason, the people you would normally not want to be associated with are coming into your cave. Look at David. His choice was to stay in a dark cave or venture outside the cave where the king and his army were searching to kill him. Have you ever been faced with choices like that? And if that does not make you angry, then try being the gathering point for every weirdo in the neighborhood. Can it get any worse?

But Saul will not let David rest and so he hounds him by chasing him throughout the countryside. Saul wasn't content to chase David out of the palace--he wants David's head on a plate. Have you ever been falsely accused? Worse, has the one who accused you followed you everywhere you go, maligning your character?

There you are in your cave trying to figure out what just

happened to you. "What went wrong?" you cry out. After all, you have this tremendous prophetic word given to you, but how is it going to happen now? It doesn't look like you will ever be king. Hey, maybe you were just too happy living at the palace. Maybe the rumors got out that your destiny was to be king and somehow Saul heard and tried to end your life. Maybe you were climbing the corporate ladder too fast. What did I do that was wrong?

To make things worse, *"all those who were in distress or in debt or discontented gathered around him, and he became their leader,"* (1 Samuel 22:2). That's right, when you are falsely accused and running for your life, who should gather around you? All the strange people.

But there is more! King Saul, who will not leave you alone, comes into the very cave you have been chased into and you know what he does? *"He came to the sheep pens along the way; a cave was there, and Saul went in to relieve himself. David and his men were far back in the cave,"* (I Samuel 24:3). This is what we hate and it happens to so many of us. You would think it is bad enough that he accuses you falsely or that he is hounding you trying to kill you but now he has come into your cave the very place he has harassed and driven you into and he defecates in your cave. He defecates in your cave!

If it happened to me I would be furious, yet David never lifts a finger against Saul. There is something about the character of David that is so amazing that even those men who had come into his cave, the misfits of society, saw in David something so extraordinary that it changed their lives. They became David's mighty men and did exploits that were far greater than what Saul's men had accomplished. They saw something in the character of David that so impacted them that it changed them from being misfits into being mighty.

The interesting thing about David is that he would not allow the circumstances of life to change who he was. <u>Most people would be so overwhelmed by self-pity they would react out of their hurt instead out of their promise</u>. If we allow self-pity to rule us, we never will make it out of the cave into our next election because of our attitude. How many do not go to church anymore? How many attend church but they don't do anything to serve there because they are still in the cave of self-pity?

It is true that many Christians are still living in caves and it does not matter if they were totally responsible for what happened or not. They just do not realize that they can leave the cave and walk out at any time, for their destiny still awaits.

DAVID THE KING OF JUDAH

David learned to embrace this cave trial and have a positive emotional response no matter how difficult his life's experiences could be. That is something each one of us needs to learn. No matter how difficult the circumstances have become we need to embrace our test or trial and have a positive attitude. Having a positive emotional response in any given situation is difficult. Most of the time when faced with a difficult choice we fight with the same weapons used against us. We would do better to lift the battle to a higher place and use weapons of peace, love, understanding, patience and hope. Within each person are two people; one who is ruled by his sin-nature whom we are not to resist on his own level and with his own weapons and another person who is not evil, but who can be reached by love. We need to look on the bright side, but I think all of us can admit from experience that at the time it can be a very hard thing to do.

David learned from his time spent in the cave, but he was also preparing others for the election that was coming his way. To be a cave dweller was part of the process to his destiny as king over all of Israel, and those impacted by his time in the cave were going to play an important role in both his process and his destiny.

God blessed us with free will. Since the situations that come our way are preparing us for our destiny, we need to exercise our freewill and maintain a positive attitude. Rather than pray for the mountain before us to disappear, it would be better for us to pray for the strength to make it through the mountain and stand victorious on the other side.

DAVID the KING OF ISRAEL

David came out of that cave as the King of Judah, a title he held for 7 1/2 years until he became the king over all of Israel. When he became the king of Israel, he had arrived at that place of destiny, that place that God had ordained for him. When David reached his place of destiny, it birthed something! And for David, that new birth was the lineage of the Messiah.

Why isn't the church growing in leaps and bounds? It is because so many are still in a cave still holding regrets, still angry with what happened, still upset by all that transpired that got them into the cave that they have no vision for getting out of the cave.

I wonder what would be birthed out of our lineage if we reached that place of destiny that God has prepared for us? We need to look at a bad day as an opportunity, not just an accident. If we would realize that we are so special that no one who has come before us or anyone who will come after us could ever be able do the things we are destined to do. The things we are destined to accomplish through our passing from calling to election, and then to fulfilling our destiny, will be an ever-widening ripple that will affect the lives of others throughout all of eternity. We really are history makers.

DAVID'S DESTINY and BEYOND

<u>It is very important that we realize that fulfilling our destiny can be our place of greatest challenge.</u> When David came to his place of destiny, it was there that he committed adultery and then killed Bathsheba's husband Uriah. We should learn that just because we have reached that place of destiny does not mean it is a time to rest. We read in the Bible that David did not go out to war as was his custom. David stayed home when he should have been at war. It was while he was at home that he saw Bathsheba bathing and had an affair with her.

Later, when David wanted to build the house of the Lord, God told David that his son would have the privilege because he had too much blood on his hands. David's cross as king was one that only he could carry and, when he laid it aside, he sinned against God and fell to his lowest point. Reaching your place of destiny can be your greatest challenge if you are not careful. David's greatest failing in life was the condition he left his family in because of his sin. It is hard for us to imagine what it would have been like for Israel if David would not have sinned and would have left for history a family that was healthy in every aspect.

Everyone wants to be a Daniel, but no one wants to be thrown into the lion's den! Everyone wants to be a Joseph, but no one wants to be falsely accused and then thrown into prison!

Everyone wants to be a prophet like John the Baptist, but no one wants their head on a plate!

CHAPTER 7

JOHN THE BAPTIST

When life does not turn out like you planned.

I think we can all agree that life is not easy--that there are ups and downs to the path we must travel. We think that we are unique to the problems of life and assume that if we were one of the famous people that it would somehow be much easier. Let's look at Luke 7:23. *"Blessed is the man who does not fall away on account of me."* This is a verse that seems to be out of place that it does not fit in with the rest of the discourse that is going on but it carries a very real and strong message to each one of us. This is the point where John the Baptist had been thrown into prison. Tradition tells us that he was in the lowest part of the prison where all the sewage flowed through, but we also find him at his lowest place of despair. It is at this place that we find John beginning to question what he had seen concerning Jesus.

John saw the dove come down and light upon Jesus' head when he baptized Jesus. John heard the audible voice of God say the words from heaven, *"This is my son in whom I am well pleased."* He had seen and heard all these things, but when you are at your lowest point and the feelings of self-doubt come upon you, then your imagination begins to run wild and you begin to question everything.

Even though John knew and had even said, *"He must increase and I must decrease,"* this was not exactly the "decrease" he had in mind for the end of his life. When you are in the cave or the dungeon and things are not turning out exactly as you may have imagined, you can begin to wonder about life. There came a time when John the Baptist began to doubt and in that doubt he called two of his disciples to him for he was troubled and had an assignment for them. *"Calling two of them, he sent them to the Lord to ask. 'Are you the one who was to come, or should we expect someone else,"* (Luke 7:18, 19)

That is where we find ourselves in Luke 7:20-22. John's disciples are making their way through the crowd of people surrounding Jesus. *"When the men came to Jesus, they said, John the Baptist sent us to you to ask, "Are you the one who was to come, or should we expect someone else?"* Jesus says to them, *"Go back and report to John what you have seen and heard: The blind receive sight, the lame walk, those have leprosy are cured, the deaf hear, the dead are raised, and the good news is preached to the poor."*

Then Jesus says something that is completely out of

character, for it does not seem to fit in with what just happened. But Jesus continues (verse 23), *"Blessed is the man who does not fall away on account of me."* When Jesus said this, it was not only to John's disciples but also to us as well. He said it because there are going to be times in your life in which you are going to be disappointed. <u>There are going to be times when things do not turn out the way you had thought they would.</u> Maybe you thought it was going to be you and Jesus forever going higher and higher like climbing the corporate ladder of success, just going from glory to glory. <u>You may be disappointed, but rest assured that if you continue onward, God's purposes will be fulfilled in your life.</u>

Jesus said that John the Baptist was the greatest prophet that ever walked the earth, the one who heralded the coming of Jesus the Christ. This mighty prophet died in prison because a king and his daughter during a wild party thought that it would be great sport to have John beheaded and his head put on a platter and brought before the king's dinner guests.

The fulfillment of our destiny contains within it different callings and elections that happen to us as we progress to our destiny. It is our emotional response to those situations that make all the difference as to whether or not we make it to that place of destiny.

Are we going to internalize everything that has happened and remain imprisoned by our reaction to a circumstance? Or are we going to be able to emotionally embrace a positive response to past situations so we can be free to come out of the cell and into the next election that is awaiting us? It is our own choices, not our circumstances, that have come to define our identity. Regardless how bad our living environment is, or how humiliating and degrading others have been to us, we are still in control of how we choose to respond.

Our free-will gives us the ability to have a good attitude while doing what is right in the midst anything the world offers us, whether it good or evil. That is one thing Satan can never take from us. He can take our life, he can throw us in prison, he can have all our friends come against us, but he can never take away our free-will. God wants us to run the race of life with a good heart and an equally good attitude. That is what brings glory to our Lord and Savior.

It drives Satan crazy that when you are hated, despised, and nailed to a cross that you react not like the world would react, but like Jesus. Only Jesus' love can empower us to look at those who did this and with complete surrender say, "Forgive them, for they know not what they do."

CHAPTER 8

OUT OF CONTROL

Falling isn't hard--it's the sudden stop that will kill you.

I have met Christians that believe that Jesus went to the cross like a defeated man, but he was not defeated. Peter says, *"His divine power has given everything we need for life and godliness,"* (II Peter 1:3). We do not live a defeated life nor do we follow a defeated king, but we live a positive life understanding that everything that happens to us has a divine purpose.

Peter wants us to know that everything that happened to him had to happen so that he could come to the end of his "self". Even after all that Peter had been involved with for those three years with Jesus, the self-life was still big within Peter. Self-pride and self-justification played a big role in Peter's life and Peter had to come to the end of all of that "self" so that he could truly become what God intended him to be.

This is what was within Peter, even though on the outside he was a man of complete surrender to the call of God on his life. On the outside, Peter was a man of perfect submission to whatever God had for him to do. Peter was the one who demonstrated immense faith and walked on water when Jesus beckoned him come and he was the one who had incredible spiritual vision in declaring Jesus was the "Son of the living God!"

The truth was that, consciously or subconsciously, Peter was taking all the credit for doing "great things" for the kingdom. Jesus had to bring him to the end of himself so that Peter would realize that it is all God.

Peter wants us to understand that as we successfully pass from our callings through our elections that it will eventually lead us to our destiny. He writes this passage to encourage us, that if we grasp what he is telling us we will not fall as he did. *Webster's Dictionary* defines the word fall as *to descend freely, to drop to a lower position; to lose office, to suffer ruin, defeat, or failure.* We all have read the accounts of Peter's denial of Jesus, but I wonder if we really understand what was going on inside of him?

Throughout the generations since Jesus' death and resurrection there have been countless people who have fallen within the church. I am not talking specifically about a moral failure but a loss of their destiny and purpose in Christ that left them feeling spiritually ineffective and unproductive. David could easily have thrown up his arms in the cave and given up. Joseph could have given up in prison after being falsely accused. As we begin to understand the process of calling and election leading to our destiny, we will realize that each situation in which we find ourselves, whether favorable or unfavorable, is actually an opportunity to have our will to actively align with the will of our Father.

When we attempt to create the path to our own destiny through our own strength, it may ultimately lead us to our destiny. But once we get there, we will not be as prepared as God intended us to be had we followed his plan. Only God can take the things that come our way and give us the opportunity to turn what the world would see as a demotion and turn it into a promotion. <u>Demotion is often a necessary process that we must all go through in our journey to our destiny so that our character can be changed into godliness.</u>

Our reaction to life's circumstances will ultimately shape our lives into the person God intends for us to become. All we have to do is embrace what God is doing with a positive emotional response to whatever comes our way.

In all four of the gospel accounts Peter was strong in the things of God. After Jesus told Peter he would deny him three times, Peter boldly said, *"Lord, I am ready to go with you to prison and to death."* The funny thing about that statement is that he meant every word of it! He even had one of the swords that Jesus told them to get and when the time came for him to use it on the Mount of Olives, he took it and cut off the servant's ear. (See Luke 22:36). As soon as Peter cut the man's ear off, Jesus looked at Peter and rebuked him by saying, *"No more of this!"* Things were not going well for Peter that night. First, Jesus tells him Satan has asked to sift him as wheat and that he would deny Jesus not once but three times. Even after he responded by saying that he is ready to die for Jesus, he was bold enough to have picked up one of the swords that Jesus told them they should have. Then when he used it to cut the ear off the servant he got rebuked by Jesus for doing what he thought he was supposed to do. After all that, Peter was still the one who followed Jesus into the courtyard after his arrest. Peter had guts. Even in his greatest moments of self-doubt and uncertainty, Peter was at least there with Jesus.

Being in the courtyard was not an easy thing for Peter. He was a man of action and the longer he sat in the courtyard, the more he thought about all that transpired throughout the night. The more Peter thought about it, his self-confidence in his ability to control everything began to crumble. Things were not supposed to happen like this. Peter thought he had it all figured out and now he was not so self-assured. He did not like what had happened, but as he looked around him he could not see one friendly face. And the faces of those who were looking in his direction were not very friendly at all. For the first time, his self-boasting about who he was and what he could do began to waver inside of him and his desire for self-preservation began to take over.

Often people would recognize the men that were with Jesus by the accent they had when they spoke. They were Galileans and they spoke differently than most of the people that were around them. I live near Philadelphia and people in east Philly speak differently than anyone else in our nation. When I think of Jesus' disciples and how they had this accent and this rough way of acting and talking, I imagine they sound a lot like the guys I met down on the streets in east Philadelphia.

Peter wandered around in the courtyard and tried to find out what was happening to Jesus. I imagine he does not even see her, but out of nowhere a servant girl comes up to him and says, *"You were also with that Nazarene, Jesus."* Peter denies it. *"I don't know or understand what you are talking about,"* he answered. (See Mark 14:67-68). Maybe it was part of Peter's self-preservation or maybe he just didn't know what to say and that was the first thing that came out of his mouth. I do not know how I would have responded. Peter certainly would have been experiencing a little fear mixed with some high anxiety and it's possible he responded to the servant girl off the top of his head, without thinking.

If I was Peter and I was in that crowd, it wouldn't have taken much to convince me that there were a lot of people hanging around there and not many of them were my friends. Maybe he was lost in thought about the incident of cutting off the servants ear or perhaps he was going over the conversation with Jesus when he said, *"Satan has asked to sift you as wheat."* Maybe it was an innocent thing, perhaps there was not much thought involved with his first denial. He may have self-justified it as being just an innocent thing to say to deflect all of the stares and whispers coming from those around him. He had bigger problems and with that kind of thinking, you can self-justify many of your actions.

Peter wanted to put some distance between him and the girl so he got up from where he was sitting and went over and stood by a doorway. He felt safer there, but others had overheard what the girl said and it wasn't long until someone else saw him and came over said, "This fellow is one of them." Out of the corner of his eye, Peter could see the heads begin to turn in his direction once again and Peter responds emphatically that he did not know Jesus.

Now more people became interested in Peter's involvement, and Peter saw people talking and nodding their heads toward him. Finally, a group of people close to him began to speak loudly amongst themselves and looking at Peter said, *"Surely you are one of them, for you are a Galilean."* Listen to Peter's response. *"He began to call down curses upon himself, and he swore to them, 'I don't know this man you're talking about,'"* (Mark 14:70-71). The first time he responded may have been without thinking, but things were getting out of hand. It seemed like each denial was stronger than the previous one. Peter was willing to deny Jesus not for anything other than his own self-preservation. The desire to survive was stronger than the desire to know God.

The words were hardly out of his mouth when suddenly the rooster crowed twice and he realizes the words the Lord spoke to him just hours before. Peter raises his head and he sees Jesus looking right at him as he is led through the courtyard. It was not an incriminating look, nor a look of bewilderment, but a look of understanding and love--a look that Peter would remember for the rest of his life.

For the first time, Peter began to see himself for who he really was. All his boastfulness, his pride, his arrogance was before him and nothing he could say or do could justify his actions to himself. He saw himself for what he was like and it broke him. He came to the end of himself. Not even a phony king wants to be seen for what he truly is.

As the full impact of what he did comes upon Peter, he weeps bitterly. When it says that he, "wept bitterly" it does not mean some wimpy crying. It means that from out of the depths of his inner being comes racking sobs, sobs that were gut wrenching. For probably the first time in his life, Peter was seeing himself for who he really was. *"And all our righteousness are like filthy rags,"* (Isaiah 64:6). If you have ever seen yourself for who you really are inside, or have had the true motives behind your actions exposed before you, then there are only two options left for your life. You can kill yourself because you cannot stand yourself (defeated phony king that you are) or you can resign yourself to live a life of disgrace, a shell of the man or woman you could have been.

Judas went out and killed himself but Peter chose the latter and resigned himself into exile and went back to do what he knew he was good at. After all, he was a fisherman. Who was he trying to fool? This is the place where we are keenly tempted to give up our destiny and remain in the cave, exiled to living a life of what could have been. Unlike Peter, most people have never fully recovered from their experience and are still in exile. For Peter, Jesus was there to come and rescue him from his self-exile and restore him on the path of his destiny. In doing so, Jesus actually gave to the church the ministry of reconciliation. For those that are still unable to come out of their self-exile, God is sending someone to come alongside of them to bring restoration—someone to remind them that their destiny still awaits and to encourage them to continue onward.

Those that are still in exile are living in a cell, but one in which the door is wide open. They can leave that cell behind at any time, but they cannot get the past the fact that they failed. Some want to resurrect their old kingdom back to its original glory, to get things back where it was in the beginning but still under their own terms. Others want their lives back but who would want them? And can you blame them? After all, once a failure always a failure. They just feel like they messed up so badly that there is no way God could use them now. All those prophetic words spoken over them are considered as good as gone because they will never be that person again because they feel that person no longer exists.

The sad part is that there are people within the church who will agree with you, that you are a failure or worthless. Some people convey the message clearly--you may be restored but not to the place you were before. We can forgive, but we will never forget. I read a study once that said that people in the west are hesitant in hiring someone who has failed because they feel they were way over their heads and putting them back into that situation is only asking for a repeat of that person's past performance. But those in the east would often hire those who had failed because they felt that if they had learned from their experience it made them stronger leaders and ones who were prone to not fail again.

Peter walked in that inner circle as a close friend of Jesus. Many would not say it in so many words, but when Peter fell there just might be an opening for a new close friend now. The amazing thing is that even those who were closest to you now can see clearly the reasons as to why you fell. They can see that you fell because you were arrogant and self-righteous. You strutted around like a peacock thinking you were something when really you were not anything at all, just someone who could get people in to see Jesus. Didn't you notice that when Jesus left the room, no one paid any attention to you? <u>It is a sad saying but true: "Everyone wants you to do better, just not better than them!"</u>

I wonder what it is inside of people who see someone fall, but are not very anxious to run over and help pick them back up. You would think that someone nearby in the church would encourage them and tell them they are there for them and will not desert them. This is the point in which so many people leave the church. Who would want a phony like them around? Have you ever wondered what happened to people that used to sit beside you week after week? The enemy came in like a flood and took them out and we just sat back and made a decision, consciously or unconsciously, not to do anything to help them.

There is something that we need to learn from Peter's story. First of all, usually what happens to us will happen in threes as it did with Peter. Think about it. Peter's first denial would not have had Peter come to the end of himself, nor the second denial. But when it came to three denials in a row, it was more than Peter could bear. I'm sure he could hear Jesus' words in his mind.

"Satan has asked to sift you like wheat! Like Wheat!" Maybe you can see a pattern beginning to emerge, that what happened to Peter can or has happened in your life. It begins innocently enough. Your car breaks down, making you late for work. Even though you have never been late before, this was the wrong day to show up late. Your boss just told everyone this morning that because so many people have been late for work that the next person that walks through the door late is going to be fired. You walk in and even though this is the first time you were ever late your boss says he is sorry but he must stand by what he said. Dazed you begin to head home, your car is broken, you have just lost your job, and you go and do the last thing you would have ever thought of doing when you woke up this morning. And for an reformed alcoholic it is the worst thing you could do. Each thing builds on the next until you see that you are your own worst enemy.

We are not the enemy, but there is a real enemy out there that wants to maim, kill and destroy, and it is the devil. The devil will use anything he can to accomplish his goal. His main goal is for you to serve him, but if that is not possible and you do accept Jesus as your Savior, he will do everything he can to stop you from allowing Jesus to be Lord over your life. If he can stop this from happening, then the civil war that will wage within you will cripple you from ever living the abundant life that is mentioned in John 10:10.

The old king is ruled by your sin nature. The sin-nature is the desire to be equal to or superior to God. We were born into sin. We had no choice in this, because when Adam and Eve sinned, sin entered into the world. The old king rules over a dysfunctional kingdom that is always in disarray. The counsel the old king receives is from the areas of your life where "self" rules. To some degree the situations that have happened in your life have shaped you into the person you have become. If you have lived in poverty or wealth, been neglected or showered with attention, grew up as an orphan or adopted, all these things have shaped you into the person you have become. But consider for a moment that the old king, your old nature, is not that sympathetic to what has happened in your life. The old king is more interested in using those very circumstances to further entrench his position to rule and reign in your life. Each of the damaged areas in your life becomes the counsel the old king uses as guidance in the decisions he makes for you. No wonder your life can be so difficult.

That is why when Jesus becomes Lord of your life he does not do away with your "self" but redeems it by your willfully giving it over to the new King. This is the process of dying to "self" so that "self" can be resurrected into the glory that our Father has destined it to be since the beginning of time.

Often the attack will not be as easy as one, two, three. It can come upon you suddenly and out of nowhere. Imagine you are standing knee deep in the ocean and you are looking out watching the waves coming in. If you can see a big wave coming you can prepare yourself for it so that it has little effect on you. Now turn around and face the land. This is what it is like when the enemy comes in like a mighty flood. A wave comes in and completely overwhelms you. There is no time to take a deep breath, no time to brace yourself or dive into the wave and swim under it, the wave tumbles you down and down until your lungs are about to explode and you feel like you are going to die. Your mind is whirling as you try to figure if you are heading further down or if you are swimming toward the surface. You're completely disorientated emotionally, physically and spiritually.

When this happens, there are periods of calm when it seems like things are coming back to normal but then another waves hits you, then another. You know that what is happening is an attack of the enemy but you do not know when it will come and when it does it overwhelms you to such a degree that you actually find yourself being taken along by all the doubts, fears, insecurities, and trauma. You struggle to survive by blaming yourself or others. Survival is strong within each one of us and the will to live is powerful. If it was one wave you could easily survive it, but when it comes upon you wave after wave then you feel like you are losing your mind. You try to find out if there are any open doors in your life that the enemy would have that kind of foothold over you. Oftentimes there is someone close to you or someone you barely know cursing you in some way. You search your heart, pray, cry out to God, accuse those close to you, check your diet, any medication you are on or vitamin you are taking and wait. Will the last wave that hits you be the last or is there another one coming that will hit you when you least expect it? The battle for your mind is here and the enemy is fast approaching.

You may be reading this right now and have gone through this yourself or know someone who has. Some may be saying that they have never experienced anything like this and cannot think of anyone who has. Often when someone is going through this, they isolate themselves from everyone so that no one will see them in this state. The last think they need is for someone to think or tell them that they are losing their minds. If this has not happened to you and you feel like it never would, then be careful. Pride does come before the fall. After all, look at Peter's life.

This kind of attack is more common that many of us realize and it reaches down to the very depths of our human understanding. It makes you feel like the sand beneath your feet is sinking and your reality has been shifted, sending you into a free-fall. It is at this time when you feel alone, utterly alone. That is why we need each other to encourage, edify, and build each other up until this crashing wave has passed. Many times these attacks come before a major breakthrough in your life. It is the enemy's attempt at stopping you from stepping into the promises of God, promises that are just around the corner.

Peter's problems may not have seemed so big, but the roots underneath his denials went to the very core of his ego. The wave hit Peter and he went out weeping bitterly. We really do not know what Peter went through after that initial wave, but I am sure there were other waves of doubts, anguish, fears and anger that swept over him. His world was just turned upside down, and every time he surfaced another wave seemed to send him to the bottom once again.

CHAPTER 9

THE MINISTRY OF RECONCILIATION

Being loved back to life.

Who brought Peter back from his self-imposed exile? Jesus! And when Jesus showed up and invited Peter to come to him, he also invited the church to come to him. It was at this moment in time that Jesus introduced into the church the ministry of reconciliation.

Why do you think Peter outran John to the tomb that day? I wonder if Peter was thinking that if he could just get there first before anyone else, he could tell him how sorry he was. Peter wanted to tell him that he really did not mean it, that he was so sorry for what he had said to everyone and how empty he felt inside having said those words. Sadly, for Peter, Jesus was gone and all that was left were his grave clothes.

There was nothing left for Peter to do but to leave and go back to the only thing he was really any good at--fishing. What does Jesus do? He goes and finds Peter. Jesus did not wait until

Peter comes and apologizes, but he goes out and finds Peter. And Jesus knew just where Peter would be. When Peter sees Jesus, he jumps into the water and swims to shore to talk to him before the others can get there. When he arrives, he sees that Jesus has a fire burning and was stooped over the fire, cooking.

Peter really does not know what to say, which is surprising when you think of all the times when he just barged into the conversation and began to talk before he would even think. This time there were so many things on his heart that each one of his thoughts seemed to bump into the next until none of the words he had so carefully constructed in his mind could find their way out. Peter sat down staring into the fire trying to dry himself off from the swim he just finished, lost in a myriad of thoughts.

Jesus does not go up to the repentant and broken Peter and say, "Hey Peter! You know when that girl came up to you and said, 'Do you know me?' You told her you didn't know me and that hurt me." Jesus didn't say that. He would never say that to Peter or you. What did Jesus say? He looked over at Peter and, if Peter had looked up at that moment, he would have seen those eyes, full of love, looking down at him. Peter was too lost in his thoughts sitting beside the fire. Jesus did not go over all the denials and mistakes that Peter had made. Why? Because those mistakes and the denials burned within him every day. Peter rehashed them repeatedly in his mind a thousand times a day since it first happened, living in the self-imposed hell that his life had now become.

It is sad that many of us perhaps even right now continually revisit that place where we fell. We go there so often that we have come to relive it repeatedly thinking of all the promises and failures and the "what could have been". Our life has become the old soap opera, "As the World Turns," and the familiar line goes through our minds, "As the sand goes through the hour glass, so do the days of our lives." We just see the sand pouring through and it seems so hopeless. That old king inside sees no hope either. That is how Satan wants it to be for us. Thankfully, we have a new King that lives within us and it is at these crucial times in our lives when he comes and finds us as he did with Peter.

Jesus looked down at Peter and asks, *"Simon son of John, do you truly love me more than these?"* Peter may have been lost in thought much like he was when he sat around the fire in the outer courtyard. Perhaps he heard the words Jesus spoke to him and without looking up he responded by saying, *"Yes, Lord, you know that I love you."*

Then Jesus spoke to Peter a second time, *"Simon son of John, do you truly love me?"* Perhaps that took Peter back to that second place where he had denied Jesus. Maybe with a little more forcefulness, with a little more resolve in his manner Peter could not change what he had said then, but he could say what he felt now. Looking up at Jesus, Peter said, *"Yes, Lord, you know that I love you."*

Then Jesus took Peter to that third place and asked Simon, not Peter, *"Simon son of John, do you love me?"* It hurt Peter, because Jesus asked him a third time. Then Peter, looking deep into the face of Jesus' eyes, those same eyes that he had seen when he looked across the courtyard after the rooster crowed and with all the tears and sorrow in his heart Peter replied, *"Lord, you know all things; you know that I love you."* The most important thing that mattered in the entire world came back before Peter and it was not about his failure it was not about his denial, it was about his love for Jesus.

Peter wrote this so that what happened to him does not have to happen to anyone else. But if it has happened to you, then you will know what to do. And if it happens to someone you know, then you now know how to get them out their self-imposed exile. You do not do it by blaming them or accusing them. No one could blame them anymore than they have been blaming themselves. You take them to the resurrected Jesus, the one standing victorious and strong, and have them look into his eyes and encourage them to have a talk with Jesus. Encourage them to let Jesus love the life back into them!

There will be times in our lives when we will come to the realization that our walk with God is not as it should be. Perhaps there have been times in your life when you have found yourself in a dry and thirsty place in your walk with Jesus and you feel like you have been walking alone. It is at those times that we feel like the old king has come once again into our lives and slowly taken over once again. We find ourselves tired of trying to manage our lives, trying to do everything and do it right.

We are in need of a revival of His presence in our lives, a fresh infusion of His love. We need to return to Jesus His right to rule and reign over our lives and having given that right back into His hands we need to listen to His voice and return to that valley where we can be pruned once again so we may produce the fruit worthy of his love.

Peter knew there must be a better way to come to the end of oneself than crashing and burning along life's highways. We can easily talk about the self-pride and the self-confidence that was in Peter. It is all rooted in that one word, "self". Christ says to us, "Deny Self," and like Peter, we may never have understood or obeyed. Jesus watched over Peter and brought him to that place where self, had to be exposed and disposed.

We may think that once we have come to the end of ourselves that the battle is over, but that is far from the truth and Peter realized it. Peter knew that the old king would try to come and re-establish his right to rule and reign. If there was one thing Peter learned, it was that he could not really trust himself to make sound decisions all the time. Peter was humbled, but to keep his humility meant he had a very real understanding of what he was capable of becoming once again. Perhaps the words that are the opposite of humble will tell us something about what Peter never wanted to become again:

- Arrogant
- Conceited
- Egotistical
- Haughty
- Pompous

We need to remember how far Peter had fallen and how badly he never wanted that to happen again. He knew the dangers and he knew if that sly old king was given any room, he would return. We do not need to go through what Peter went through. He realized it too late, but that did not mean it had to happen to others either. Years later, Peter was in his cell and he put pen to paper and remembered the words Jesus said to him: *"And when you have turned back, strengthen your brothers,"* (Luke 22:31). And Peter began to write.

PART - 2

SIGNS YOU CANNOT AFFORD TO MISS!

Introduction

When I first began working on this part of the message, I struggled to find an appropriate title. I began with "Eight Steps to a Fulfilled Life." It didn't take long before I realized that others, including me, really did not like taking "eight steps" to anything. That led me to the next title, "Going from Glory to Glory." I decided that one was better, but I was not entirely happy with it so I finally changed it to, *The Journey to Your Destiny*.

I have come to the conclusion that it's not that we don't like journeys or steps, it's that we don't like it when we think the steps require effort. And we really don't like it when the journey takes longer than a short stroll! We want the immediate, effortless, non-changing approach to attaining the character of Christ. There have been times in my life when God has blessed me with a supernatural transformation that happened inside of me that was instantaneous. I must admit that I prefer that method of receiving change to any other method, but I realize that's the exception and not the rule.

Even though we all have an incredible destiny and purpose to our lives, getting to that place is often difficult and tiresome, but it is worth the journey. In life we will encounter good times and bad times. We do live in a fallen world. Whether the situations we encounter in life are good or bad, following the "eight signs" that Peter has laid out for us will ensure that we will get through the problems with style and grace.

Most of the battles we will face are not moral problems, but they are problems nonetheless. I should know--I have battled my fair share and I will continue dealing with areas of my life that I want to see changed. The truth of the matter is that I can go through life with these flaws or I can deal with them. The alternative is to not deal with them and let them be passed down to my children and grandchildren. We can pass down a legacy of money and fame, but if that is all we have to give then we should be pitied all the more. But I believe it is more important to pass on the spirit of an overcomer who came into his inheritance as a laid down lover of God.

CHAPTER 10

FAITH

Standing Differently

Peter left us eight sign posts that if followed will give us the shortest route in reaching our destiny. Each of the eight signs gives us the direction we need to reach our destination. Faith leads to goodness, knowledge, self-control, perseverance, godliness, brother kindness and love. I cannot stress how important it is that we understand that as we journey through life we will pass by these eight signs many times. The signs give us direction, but they also inform us of what we are currently going through. They also speak of a process that we must journey through if we are to arrive at the destination.

The first sign we find on our journey is "faith". *Webster's Dictionary* defines faith as *the firm belief in something for which there is no proof.* Further along it says that faith is *the belief and trust in and loyalty to God.* I would say it is all that and more! Yes, it is the belief in something that you cannot prove; but it is also firmly believing, trusting, and being loyal to God. When I accepted Jesus as my Savior, I did so by exercising my faith. I used to say that when I received Jesus as my Savior, I put all my eggs in one basket--either this is it or there is nothing. There was no plan "B".

After I accepted Jesus, I went to bed that night not really feeling much different than I previously had felt. That was about to change because I awoke to a new reality within me, one that was totally foreign to what I had previously known. During the night, I had gone through a transformation that was as drastic as if I had gone from a black and white to a colored world. I am not sure how I knew things were different, even now I have troubled articulating just how I knew, but the reality was this-- three things I had struggled with for most of my life were gone, sovereignly taken away.

How did I know things had changed? I had not really talked to anyone or really had a chance to interact in any setting with a group of people, yet I knew things were different. It was like the times when I would walk outside in the fall and felt the first whisper of fall in the air or when a warm breeze came by after a long winter that reminded you of the warmth of spring. It was not that the weather had changed dramatically but somehow you just knew a change had taken place.

Within me there was a slight perception that a shift had taken place and things were different. That is what I felt on the inside.

A shift had taken place and I knew I was not the same person. I knew that this change had to do with the prayer I said the night before, I knew it had to do with Jesus. There was more to my giving my heart to Jesus than I realized. I was experiencing "faith".

I do not know if any one of us fully grasps the transformation that occurs when we accept Jesus as our Savior. Jesus describes it like this in John 3:3. *"I tell you the truth, no one can see the kingdom of God unless he is born again."* Nicodemus replied, *"How can a man be born when he is old? Surely he cannot enter a second time into his mother's womb to be born!"*

Like Nicodemus, we struggle to fully grasp the significance of what Jesus meant. Even though all of us have experienced natural birth, I do not know of anyone who can remember exactly what it felt like when they were born. Even though we understand that being born or dying is but a transformation from one reality to another, none of us can fully understand or really explain what that must feel like. Yet Jesus tells us that when we humble ourselves and by faith ask Jesus to come into our lives, there is a transformation that takes place within us that is comparable to passing from one reality to another--that's the experience of being born again.

When we accept Jesus into our lives by faith, it transforms us into a different person and gives us the ability to stand differently. The old nature, or the way we viewed life before Christ, has been given over to a completely new nature and with it we find ourselves positioned in a much different direction. Before it was all about us and what we could get out of life, but now we begin to see life in an entirely new and refreshing way.

When we confess our faith in Jesus Christ as being our Lord and Savior, we seldom have a complete understanding of what that really means. It causes us to experience something so far outside our ability to understand that we are in effect saying, "I will hope in something other than what I can do myself." What we have experienced because of faith in God rather than ourselves is beginning to affect our character. As our character changes, our conduct will change.

Because of the change in our stance, our whole being cries out within us that this is the path we have searched for our entire life. The answer to the question, "Who am I?" is now finding its answer in "I am a child of the King!" We are now experiencing what we call new birth or being born again, not my physical means but by spiritual. We now have the ability to see the good in life because we are seeing life through an entirely different paradigm. Our previous way of looking at things was filtered through the lenses of our own selfish reasoning--our sin nature.

Our sin nature is what every one of us receives when we are born into this world. It was our nature to sin. In Isaiah 64:6 the prophet says, *"All our righteous acts are like filthy rags."* Isaiah is saying that within each person even our most righteous and moral acts are done for purely selfish reasons. In Hebrews 11:6 the writer says this, *"And without faith it impossible to please God, because anyone who comes to him must believe that he exists and that he rewards those who earnestly seek him."* Sinning has become our second nature. When we say it is "second nature to us," that means that something has become so well-developed and well-practiced that it seems to be completely natural.

The root of our sin nature is in the belief that equality with God is something to attain. Adam and Eve bit into and swallowed the deception that Satan presented. *"For God knows that when you eat of it your eyes will be opened, and you will be like God, knowing good and evil,"* (Genesis 3:5) "You will be like God," is quite a statement. *Equality with God* is the root of our sin nature. That is why Jesus, the second Adam, declared, *"Who, being in very nature God, did not consider equality with God something to be grasped,"* (Philippians 2:6).

We are born with the desire to be our own savior and lord over our own lives. After all, who needs God if we ourselves are a "god"? When our kingdom begins to fall apart, the self-made-king cries out for someone to save him from destruction. This self-made-king, or King-self, will not except help from anyone. So even in this state, his ego will not accept any help from anyone other than another king. This really describes the situation in which most individuals find themselves when they come to accept Jesus as their Savior. King-self has lost control of his kingdom and cries out for someone to save him. However, the old king does not realize that this new king is the Holy King and he comes with a holy and righteous kingdom.

Within the heart of every person born there is throne, a God throne, which is a place where God is supposed to reign in every individual. It is sad that even though we were born with this throne within us, we are not born with God sitting on it.

What had transpired in my life after accepting Jesus as my Savior was that a new kingdom had come into my life. It is a kingdom that contained everything my heart had desired since birth, for it was etched, deep within my DNA. That is why we experience such peace when we finally relinquished our right to rule and reign in our lives and give that right over to our Savior and Lord, Father and King, Redeemer and Live Giver.

Having our self as king is foreign to everything that is within us and is in effect very unnatural to us. Having Jesus as our Lord and King is very natural to us and feels like we have finally come home--that everything will be right and good as was in the beginning. Having faith in God causes us to be born again, passing from our old sin nature to a new godly nature.

CHAPTER 11

GOODNESS

Seeing Differently

The next signpost is "goodness" and it is changing how we look at the world and life. Faith gives us a new stance and enables us to look at life in a very different manner than we previously experienced. On the inside, we are changing dramatically as our spirit for the first time begins to experience life in a very different way. Previously we had been experiencing life through the lenses of our self-effort or self-righteousness, but now we are seeing through the lenses of God's righteousness, which is focused through the lenses of his goodness.

Because we now have Christ within, we are able to partake of the perfect happiness that God possesses. And what God possesses, he now wants his children to possess as well. He desires that each of us experiences his contentment and peace, and are filled with the fullness of His goodness.

Possessing God's goodness helps people not only have

righteous actions, but a righteous attitude. It is not enough that we outwardly do the right thing, but that we are right inside as well. <u>Goodness has to do with an inward contentment that cannot be affected by the circumstances of life. We find ourselves becoming partakers of the divine nature of God.</u> (See 2 Peter 1:4).

Because we are now able to see and interpret the situations of life through the lenses of His goodness, our selfish motives become even more glaring to us. We find ourselves through faith not only standing differently but, with his goodness, we see differently as well. As this happens, we begin to question our thoughts and actions that we previously took for granted.

I remember this time well for it was during this time that I had contracted to do an addition to a bank parking lot. I had run out of the right size steel rebar to put into the forms, so I substituted a lesser grade of rebar and went ahead with pouring the concrete. Later that day one of the board members of the bank that was supervising the new construction stopped by and while talking to me noticed the rebar that was extending out of the current pour of concrete. He noticed it was not the right size and asked me about it, I told him that I had ran short and it was just in this small section and not in the entire slab. I was worried that I might have to remove the entire slab and put the right size rebar back into it, so to protect myself I lied. Self-justification was so strong within me that I justified my actions and excused away my carelessness so I would not be held accountable for what I had done. After he left I found myself filled with remorse, something that a few months previously I would not have felt.

Because of my new stance, I saw things differently and I did not want to put in jeopardy what God had so graciously done in my life. I went home and all the time while eating dinner with Lois, I felt that I had to make this right or I would risk sliding further back into a place that I was glad was gone. After telling Lois what I had done, I drove nine miles back into town, went up to the man's front door, and knocked on it. He was surprised to see me at the door and asked me to come in. I walked in and in front of him and his wife and told them that I was a new Christian and that what I had told him that day was a lie. I had ran out of the right rebar to use and substituted a lesser grade rebar through a much larger part of the slab than I had led him to believe. I admitted I had done it intentionally and was sorry and if he would like I would remove everything and do it over. We talked and he asked me some questions in which I answered honestly and he decided that it would still be structurally sound and would let it go but not to let it ever happen again. I left relieved, but left that conversation with a resolve to never tell another lie again. I never wanted to be put in the situation where I had to go to an individual's house and apologize for lying. It was definitely easier to do the right thing in the first place and never lie again.

The reason I went and apologized was because of the

"goodness" that had been added to my faith. In Matthew 19:17 Jesus says, *"There is only one who is good!"* He was speaking of God, of course. What is it about "goodness" that gives us such insight into the nature of our Father in Heaven? Goodness is more than having a good moral character because it speaks of an excellence of character that is so deeply etched within us that is has to be an inherited quality. When we describe God as being "good" it is because that is who he is.

This "goodness" is the quality that each one of us would have inherited naturally from our Father had sin not entered into the picture. We must be born again to bring us back to that place where the DNA of our Father is once again within us. As Jesus, the second Adam, says in John 14:10, *"Believe me when I say that I am in the Father and the Father is in me."* He explains further in verse 20, *"On that day you will realize that I am in my Father, and you are in me, and I am in you."* Now that we understand that true, undefiled goodness is only acquired through our being born again, we must also realize that it must be consciously maintained, often in spite of the temptations and evil influences that are continually around us.

I realize that there are many men and women in the world who are not Christians, but who consider themselves to be morally good. Their standard is based on a worldly goodness that has at its core a code of ethical conduct or "moral excellence" that is based either on a fear of being caught, shamed, or punished.   They keep themselves in line by fear of punishment or a desire to be rewarded rather than by their being good because it was in his their very nature to be good.

Through the scriptures we have come to understand that God is good all the time. We also have read that before the fall Adam and Eve possessed a quality of character that carried the same degree of goodness that God their Father possessed.

We read in the book of Isaiah that, *"All our righteous acts are like filthy rags!"*   The reason our righteous acts are viewed in this manner is that at the core of all our self-righteousness is a self-centered reason for what we have done. Our old nature led by king-self takes all the credit for anything that is done within the kingdom of self except for failure. Before time began, all honor and praise was to be given to the King of Kings, and because our sin nature is such that we must rule over our kingdom, we must take what rightfully belongs to the King of Kings and keep it for our own self-gratification.

The New Covenant that was ushered in by Jesus death and resurrection has opened up a way for our Father to come and live within us. By the Holy Spirit, God imparts to all who believe access to his goodness. His goodness consists of righteousness, holiness, justice, kindness, grace, mercy, and love. Through our faith in Jesus, our Father now lives within us by the Holy Spirit. The goodness of his character suddenly and radically transforms us on the inside, affecting every fiber of our being. Finding ourselves faced in a different direction, we see life differently and it changes the way we think. Ephesians 1:18 says, *"The eyes of your heart may be enlightened in order that you may know the hope to which he has called you,"* The *goodness* of God is the sum total of all his attributes and it has been added to our *faith*, changing the way we stand and how we see everything around us.

CHAPTER 12

KNOWLEDGE

Reasoning Differently

When we accept Jesus as our Lord and Savior, we are immediately ushered into a new kingdom. As we enter that new kingdom, a transformation occurs. The clothing that we once wore that defined who we were in the old kingdom has supernaturally been removed. *"We have taken off the old self with its practices and have put on the new self, which is being renewed in knowledge in the image of its Creator,"* (Colossians 3:9-10). Our "old self" has been replaced with a "new self", which causes us to stand, look, and reason in an entirely different manner than we had previously experienced. In Colossians 3:12 we are told, *"Clothe yourselves with compassion, kindness, humility, gentleness and patience."*

This points us to the third signpost on our journey, which is *knowledge*. This is not the kind of knowledge that comes through experience or thought, which is capable only of producing self-pride. Paul tells us about this kind of knowledge in I Corinthians

8:1-2. *"We know that we all possess knowledge. Knowledge puffs up, but love builds up. The man who thinks he knows something does not yet know as he ought to know. But the man who loves God is known by God."* The knowledge that Peter is talking about is knowledge that affects our will. It is knowledge of the heart, not just the mind alone. We acquired this within us as the Holy Spirit reveals the Father to us through creation, our conscience, history, providence and through the Word of God.

When Jesus came into our heart and took his rightful place as our Lord and King, we became aware that not only was he a holy king, but his kingdom was also a holy kingdom. We also became profoundly aware that what was transpiring within us was not always manifesting itself outwardly in a way that was acceptable to this new standard. *Faith* gave us the opportunity to stand in this new holy kingdom and his *goodness* gave us the ability to see things differently. Now *knowledge* has given us the ability to process the information in a totally different manner than we had previously known.

Knowledge enables us to process and understand information differently. We find ourselves in a new kingdom with a new stance. Our new nature enables us to see things in a very different way than we had previously experienced. Our ability to understand comes from the new principles acquired by our new nature. Filtered through the compassion, kindness, humility, gentleness and patience that comprise our new nature, we process information in an entirely different manner than we previously experienced.

"But wisdom is proved right by her actions," (Matthew 11:19). Knowledge may have given us wisdom, but unless we act on that wisdom it becomes of no use to us. Now we need to change the way in which we react to the situations that come our way. No matter if the situation is from our past, present, or some future event, we need to react not out of our old nature but out of the new nature that we are now in.

We need to realize that the old habits of reacting to situations cannot be allowed to continue. We need to be wide-awake and conscious of what is happening around us and especially what is happening within us. Instead of finding ourselves overwhelmed by the situations of life, we can overwhelm the situations that come our way because of Christ who lives within us.

Not only can we intentionally understand the situations we find ourselves in, but we can react to them in a totally different manner. We are now able to find ourselves not ignorant of the ways of man, the enemy, or ourselves. We can evaluate situations based on prior experience, but with our new ability to reason we do not have to fall victim to following our old ways of reacting to the situations of life.

We are often naive as to how entrenched those old patterns of reacting to crisis have become. Even reacting to everyday situations in a correct manner can become at times highly frustrating. Many of the problems that arise are because the habits of our old self impede our new nature's desire to establish new ways of reacting to situations.

For instance, I was thirty-one years old when I accepted Jesus into my life. Those thirty-one years of being my own king left me with a severely damaged system of responses to daily situations that came up in my life. Even though I knew that I needed to react to problems differently, I struggled with overcoming habits of reacting to situations because they had become so firmly entrenched within me. The reality is that all of us will have to go through the process of retraining our mind in how to process and respond differently to the situations of life.

Even though I stood differently, I saw differently, and I reasoned differently, I still needed self-control to help me change the negative patterns. My mother used to call the old patterns of thinking as "stinking thinking" and that kind of old way of looking at things needed to be changed. I really wanted to change. I did not like who I had become, and when I saw through my new nature just how messed up I really was, I knew for certain that I needed to change.

It is sad when you realize that most of the church throughout history has wanted to change, the people just didn't find the self-control and perseverance needed to enter into that place of victory.

Most people know they need to change and if you would ask them they would probably say, "Yes, I know I need to change, I admit it." Which would lead you to ask. "How are you doing after thirty years of being a Christian?" They would reply, "Well, I am more convinced now than ever that I need to change. I really feel strong about this."

Many have said, "I am a new creature in Christ all the old things have passed away." This is true, but how much of the old nature may still be present within? Look at Peter. How many times did he argue with the others over who was the greatest in the kingdom? How many times did he say things out of the mind of man and not the mind of Christ?

How many times have we found ourselves, like Peter, being satisfied in so many areas of our life? We need to realize that if we are going to change we must make a conscious decision to change. Fortunately for us there is another sign post on the horizon--*self-control*.

CHAPTER 13

SELF-CONTROL

Reacting Differently

B<i>lessed are those who hunger and thirst for righteousness, for they shall be satisfied,</i> (Matthew 5:6). Because of our new nature, we possess within ourselves a passionate desire, a holy ambition to obey, honor, and glorify God by becoming holy as he is holy.

Self-control is the signpost where probably 90% of the church is encamped. They know they need to change and they have every intention of doing so but change is hard, if not impossible, to follow through to its conclusion. That is why we need to look at the other side of the sign marked *self-control* and see the word, *perseverance*. Otherwise, we will find the old adage to be true, that the road to hell is paved with good intentions.

To exercise self-control is the innate ability to hold back the impulses that once ruled us. Self-control is the ability to control our desires and emotions while holding our rights, claims, and interests in check. <u>Self-control is the process of dying to the old nature, enabling us to react differently to any situation that may come our way. To act in true righteousness is to exercise godly willpower over all that you do.</u>

Theologians use the terms "sanctification" and "a second work of grace". When we recognize a problem in front of us, but make an intentional decision to walk through that problem to Christ-likeness, we are on the journey of sanctification and grace. When I was first saved, I was tired of my old life and really wanted a new life. I believed that Christianity held the keys to my personal happiness and would save me from continually making foolish mistakes in life. I was tired of living on a roller coaster of emotional responses as I dealt with life's situations.

I was saved in a Church that had a strong emphasis toward holiness and evangelism. They were strong on teaching us Biblical doctrines concerning the subjects of holiness and evangelism. In fact, I had come to know the Lord through a program the church used called "Evangelism Explosion," which gave you practical tools in which to present the gospel without getting side tracked in presenting the gospel message. Evangelism Explosion was exceptional in helping individuals present the gospel in a clear and concise way. Many people, including myself, came to know Jesus as their Savior through this program.

However, teaching us how to walk and live in holiness was an entirely different story. It was never their intention, but it became a holiness that was based on works. It was not so much that you were to overcome your problems as you were to control or manage your problems. I came to realize that it was like holding down a bunch of balloons under water. No matter how hard you tried every now and then one of them would pop to the surface and embarrass you. You never really got rid of them; you just learned to manage them well and keep them out of sight.

I remember once when one of my issues, uncontrollable rage and anger, got away from me and all of a sudden popped up. I remember thinking, *I thought I had that under control?* Of course, my second thought was, *Maybe control isn't what needs to happen, perhaps it would be best if it was entirely gone.*

Jesus said in Luke 14:26, *"He who does not hate...yes, even his own life...he cannot be my disciple."* What does Jesus mean when he says that I must hate my own life? It took a while, but I came to learn that the word translated "life" is "soul" the seat and center of the self-life with all its self-serving attitudes, choices, and activities.

When we received Jesus as our Savior, he gave us the ability to stand, see, and think differently. Now we are able to see how self-centered we used to be in our decision making processes. Let us face it; we would not have any need for a Savior if there were not anything from which we needed to be saved. Most of us needed to be saved not only from ourselves but also from the consequences that resulted from our faulty decisions. We have consciously and unconsciously come to not trust our decision making abilities based on how badly we did in the past. We need godly counsel and a fresh way of thinking. We need to exercise self-control to make sure that our old habits are put to death and new godly habits are put in their place.

The old-self was a shadow of what God originally planned for our lives. Even after receiving our new nature, the old unregenerate self still struggles for control. The old nature is still strong and manifests itself often. Our thoughts become consumed with old issues that were never resolved. Self-pride and self-pity argue about who did what to whom. Interestingly, I have come to realize that self-pride ends up hoisting self-pity up on his shoulders and proudly walks around showing everyone how pitiful he is, while pity cries and tells everyone that it is true, he really is the most pitiful person in the world! Self-justification joins them and finds a way to validate their arguments. Otherwise how could we live with ourselves if we were really this screwed up? These fragmented "self's" are what comprised the counsel for the old king. No wonder the old king was so confused and his kingdom collapsed. We need to be careful or we will find ourselves listening to their advice again.

These are the places where deliverance and inner healing or

so important in our walk--especially if we find we cannot overcome them on our own. Some of these areas have become strongholds in our lives and we will need help in order to overcome them. It is not a sign of weakness to ask for help. Asking for help is quite Biblical.

Why do so many great men and women of God fall? The answer is found in the life message of Peter. There is no shortcut to a life of personal holiness.

Listen, Peter fell and wept bitterly because this was as far as Peter made it in his Christian walk. Even though he completely surrendered to the call of Jesus, totally submitted to the word of God, exercised immense faith when he walked on the water, had revelatory spiritual insight into Jesus' identity, and had an incredible prophetic destiny, he still fell far short from where he needed to be.

Listen to what Paul says in I Corinthians 3:1-3: *"Brothers, I could not address you as spiritual but as worldly...mere infants in Christ. I gave you milk, not solid food, for you were not yet ready for it. Indeed, you are still not ready. You are still worldly."*

Let's look at this passage in Hebrews 5:11-14: *"We have much to say about this, but it is hard to explain because you are slow to learn. In fact, though by this time you ought to be teachers, you need someone to teach you the elementary truths of God's word all over again. You need milk, not solid food! Anyone, who lives on milk, being still an infant, is not acquainted with the teaching about righteousness. But solid food is for the mature, who by constant use have trained themselves to distinguish good from evil."*

You may be able to stand, see, and reason differently, but you need to bring everything into godly alignment. You must practice what you know to be true so that you will experience a change in behavior. This begins by exercising self-control. Beware. Self-control is dangerous if it is not aligned with the scriptures through the power of the Holy Spirit. To assume you can do it on your own, in your own power, is just the old king coming back to rule and reign, only this time he's dressed in religious robes.

Probably the best example I can think of to explain self-control is when you go on a diet. I have gone on a diet many times and I have found that it is true that cookies do talk to you. They have voices! You want to exercise self-control and get to that place of weight loss but on the journey you happen to pass by a plate of cookies and they begin to talk to you and so you pick up one--all right so you pick up two or three. It is at this place that many of us just give up on the diet all together. We just say we failed, that it is hopeless because being overweight and weak is just the way we are.

Rather than admit that we slipped, made a mistake, and go on, we just give up and quit. Self-control will never get you to the goal unless perseverance comes along side of you and stays with you until the very end. Self-control always has days when you are either doing great or days when you are struggling. It is only through perseverance will you see the changes you knew were possible. Even better, you get to see those changes become the new norm for your life.

After trying a myriad of diets I have found out that the only thing that will work in the end is watching what and how much I eat and having a lifestyle of exercising. That's not the easy answer I wanted to hear, but there are just no shortcuts with self-control and perseverance.

I have noticed that when you do lose weight everyone notices and will often comment on how well you look. They want to know how you did it because they are hoping that what you did they also can do and with the same results.

In the same way when friends and colleagues see that you are not reacting to situations in the same negative manner in which you had been doing in the past, they sit up and take notice. Our lives are not lived in secrecy. People do watch us. Many have known us since before we went to church and have taken note of any changes that have occurred since we started going.

Peter knew that self-control would not be enough. He knew that the church would need perseverance. To persevere means we have a steadfast pursuit of an aim by constant persistence. Not only do we need to react differently with self-control, but we need to persevere.

CHAPTER 14

PERSEVERANCE

Becoming Different

I do not know anyone who likes the words *self-control* or *perseverance*. But I don't know any other way to overcome something other than to begin by using self-control and perseverance until we stand on the other side, changed. It's usually during a long stretch of persevering that we find ourselves spiritually bankrupt before God. Perhaps it is in that place of spiritual poverty that we see our need for mercy for the strength to overcome—a strength that can only come from God. It's in that place of spiritual poverty that we realize how strong our will has become. It becomes clearer to us that we need our will to be in line with the will of the Father.

James says in James 1:4, *"Perseverance must finish its work so that you may be mature and complete, not lacking anything."*

Webster defines perseverance as *a continuance in a state of grace leading finally to a state of glory despite difficulties, failures, opposition or delay in achieving success.*

In spiritual terminology it is sanctification--the road to holiness or God-likeness. We are commanded to:

- Be holy (Lev. 11:44; 1 Peter 1:15-16)
- Be perfect (Matthew 5:48)
- Present your members as slaves of righteousness for holiness (Romans 6:19)

Our faith through salvation deals with the acts and guilt of committed sins, while sanctification deals with the nature of sin, the inward tendency inherited from the first Adam.

What if you became a person that exercised self-control and all of a sudden people began to see something within you that was different? People noticed that you were changing! No longer did it seem like you were just going from day to day without any conscious thought of arriving at any particular destination. Now your life seemed to have purpose, a goal. You exhibit a quiet confidence about you and people notice. You walk with a purpose, you know where you were going and how you are going to get there.

You may not have been able to put the process into words, but you are going from calling to election because you have a destiny and nothing is going to stand in the way of you attaining that which God so graciously set before for you.

Perhaps part of the problem as to why our churches are not full may be found, in part, in our lack of being people who overcome the old nature. If you go to work on Monday morning depressed and defeated and have not experienced any change in your life for 5, 10, or even 15 years, you may fool yourself but you cannot fool the people who have to live with you every day. They see that you may be great on Monday but each day after that you go downhill. You may not laugh at the off color joke, but they can see you enjoyed it and that you do more than just glance at the pin up calendar on the shop wall. Perhaps you do more than your share of gossiping. Whatever it is that has you resisting the need for change can be seen by everyone around you.

You may be able to quote all the scripture in the world, but a changed life is what people want to see. They want to see if it is possible to get out of the situation they are presently in and they are hoping, praying, that it is possible. When you are not getting better or overcoming a personal crisis, people notice. Why would they want to go to a place that doesn't have the power to change someone? If our only hope is that one day we will be in heaven, we leave the average person wanting only the opportunity to make a death bed confession because they want to have as much fun as they can until that day comes.

When they see someone who knows what they should be doing, but no power to do it, they see a person who is worse off than they are and the more to be pitied. Who would want that type of conflict in their lives? Don't they have enough troubles of their own? So they stay home, read the Sunday paper in peace, save 10% of their paycheck by not giving to the church and watch the complete football game without having to rush home or come into the game halfway through.

A person who exercises perseverance has determined that change is attainable and is worth the struggle. Perseverance says, "I will not grow weary nor will I waver in my pursuit of God. I will persistently pursue in such a way that there is resolve in my eyes that there is no turning back. I have set my face toward the prize and I will not turn to the right or the left." Webster dictionary says perseverance is *living in a continual state of grace.*

We know that the New Testament makes it clear that faith alone can save, but it also makes it equally clear that perseverance in overcoming the works of the flesh is the greatest indication than an individual's faith is genuine. (See James 2:14-26). Many times when problems come our way we pray that the mountain of adversity be removed from us rather than praying for strength to make it through the adversity and stand on the other side victorious. "Not only so, but we also rejoice in our sufferings, because we know that suffering produces perseverance; perseverance, character; and character hope," (Romans 5:3-4).

In James 1:12 it says, "Blessed is the man who perseveres under trial, because when he has stood the test, he will receive the crown of life that God has promised to those who love him." James really does not leave much doubt that if we do not persevere, we will not receive eternal life.

How many times have we read in the book of Revelation where it says, "To those who overcome!" The "those" whom Jesus is referring to are the saints of God—that's us! If we do not overcome, we will not inherit eternal life. We receive eternal life through faith but as James says in 2:17, "Faith by itself, if it is not accomplished by action, is dead." The action that James is referring to means the things that you do that mark you as dead to the old nature and alive to the new nature. In James 4:17 he says, "Anyone then, who knows the good he ought to do and doesn't do it, sins." Later he adds, "In the same way, faith by itself, if it is not accompanied by action, is dead." (James 2:17)

The entire book of James is about "perseverance." Pastors especially want their church members to be personally responsible in overcoming the problems in their own lives. Most pastors know that this is the only way to attain to the fullness that is available to us in Christ Jesus. If you really want to understand a pastor's heart for his flock, then read the entire book of James.

It is a book by a pastor to his flock. James does not hold anything from us. He speaks plainly and often forcibly, but within his words you feel his heart.

Only by our exercising self-control and continuing onward by persevering can we overcome the areas in our lives that have kept us from the abundant life. The abundant life is what Jesus promised us in John 10:10 when he said; "I have come that they may have life, and have it to the full." A full and abundant life overflows and affects every person with whom it comes in contact. You need to know that to persevere through to change will not be easy but it is worth everything.

Until we pass from this world or Jesus returns with the new heaven and earth, there will be a struggle within you between the kingdom of God and the kingdom ruled by your old self. I am not going to kid you into thinking the battle is easy, but it does get easier the more you overcome. It will seem easy when things are going great, when you're popular and everything is going you way. In reality, this is the time when the battle is the hardest and deception is at its strongest. Those are the times when it's easy to fool yourself into thinking you are popular or apparently succeeding because of what you have done or who you are. The trouble with building a God kingdom is when we do it ourselves it always crumbles. The kingdom of God is within and that is where the battle is either won or lost. It is important for us to understand there will always be an internal civil war that will rage on inside of us, each side fighting for control. This is why we must be diligent, ever confess and repent, never fully trust our motives, but search out the heart of God in all matters.

CHAPTER 15

GODLINESS

Loving Your God

*B*lessed are the pure in heart, for they shall see God, (Matthew 5:8). As we continue onward, we must continually maintain a lifestyle of exercising self-control and perseverance. As we persevere, we will see ourselves changing into *godliness*. Godliness or God-likeness is more than a breakthrough change of behavior. Godliness means we are grasping the reality and power of attaining a vital union with God. Perhaps to find its deeper meaning, we should look at the process we have experienced through this inner transformation.

Self-control and perseverance brings an inner transformation that affects our will. Our will is where our motives and attitudes find their place of origin. Our will defines who we are. Who is it that usurps God's position as Lord over our life and has the authority to compromise his authority? It is our will, the real person inside.

Our will or ego determines how much authority our Lord and King will have on the throne of our hearts. We need to guard our motives and guard our hearts:

- *"Above all else, guard your heart, for it is the wellspring of life,"* (Proverbs 4:23).
- *"As water reflects a face, so a man's heart reflects the man,"* (Proverbs 27:19).
- *"As a man thinketh in his heart, so is he,"* (Proverbs 23:7 KVJ).

When you ask Jesus into your heart as Savior and Lord, you received eternal life. Eternal life is the best "life insurance policy" you can ever receive. Whether the policy can ever be voided depends on how you interpret the fine print within the scriptures. When you accept Jesus into your life, he comes as both Savior and Lord because it is a package deal. If we would completely submit to the lordship of Jesus, things would greatly change within us. The problem is not in our desire to change, it's in the degree that our will goes along with the change. For most of us, the change is hardly noticeable at first because the will allows God only the smallest control over our lives. The will surrenders its right to rule and reign by degrees.

Adam and Eve made the "willful" decision to not trust God and become gods themselves. Genesis 3:5 shows that Satan promised them, *"You will be like God."* The choice is do we *will*fully continue to embrace the lie that we are "like God" or do we realize that we need God back on the throne of our hearts. Adam and Eve chose to *will*fully disobey God, and we now have a choice to make. Either we *will*fully submit to Jesus as our Lord or we can continue this charade and fight him every step of the way. There is a quality of life available to us if we *will*fully choose to fully trust our God. *"I am come that they might have life, and that they might have it more abundantly,"* (John 10:10 KVJ).

Purity of the heart is central to God's rule and reign in our lives. When God destroyed humankind in the days of Noah it was over the issue of the heart. *"The Lord saw how great man's wickedness on the earth had become, and that every inclination of the thoughts of his heart was only evil all the time,"* (Genesis 6:5).

The sin-nature finds its place of rule and reign in the hearts of mankind. *"For out of the heart come evil thoughts, murders, adultery, sexual immorality, theft, false testimony, slander. These are what make a man 'unclean';"* (Matthew 15:19).

Nothing shows the divisiveness of the heart more than the story of Saul. Saul was the first king over Israel. When God called Saul, he also did a transformation within his heart. In 1 Samuel 10:9 it says, *"God changed Saul's heart."* Because of the new heart that gave God him, Saul was not the same person.

However, it did not take long before Saul reverted back to his old nature of trusting in his own abilities and disobeying God. I Samuel 15:10-24 tells the story about King Saul. Saul did not carry out the Lord's instructions and he even set up a monument in his own honor. Saul was afraid of the people and gave in to them. Later, I Samuel 18:9 tell us that Saul kept a jealous eye on David. God took away the kingdom from Saul and gave it to David because Saul refused to live by the new heart God had given him. How many times in the scriptures do we read that David was "a man after God's own heart"? Psalm 78:72 says, *"He shepherded them according to the integrity of his heart, and guided them by the skillfulness of his hands."* (NKJV)

The study of David's life is a key in our understanding on how to restore our relationship with God when we make mistakes. When David was fleeing from Saul, he fled to the Philistine city of Gath. As things went from bad to worse, David became afraid and to protect himself, he began to act insane. (See 1 Samuel 21:13). Because of his outlandish behavior, the Philistines released him. While hiding in the cave of Adullum, David began to think about what had transpired and concluded that he acted dishonorable towards God by trusting in his own instincts to save himself through his own abilities rather than God's ability to protect him. It was during this time that David sat down and wrote Psalm 57 in which he declared his heart to be steadfast toward God. He rededicated his heart and repented for allowing the old king the right to think he knew more than God in how he was going to protect and preserve his own life.

Like David, we cannot allow king-self the authority to overrule our hearts commitment to God's rule and reign over our lives. Self-control and perseverance are the steps God uses to purify our heart's commitment toward Father God. This refiner's fire is the process in which our heart receives the ability to have pure motives. Pure motives are produced by being single-minded, and having an undivided and undistracted devotion to God. Perseverance produces spiritual integrity and true righteousness in our handling of the situations that life brings.

If we are not single-minded, then we are double minded. James 1:7-8 says, *"That man should not think he will receive anything from the Lord; he is a double-minded man, unstable in all he does."* James further says, *"Wash your hands, you sinners; and purify your hearts, you double-minded,"* (James 4:8). Why does James say that we should purify our hearts? Because being double-minded lets the old king back upon the throne of our hearts. *"No one can serve two masters; for he will hate the one and love the other, or he will hold to one and despise the other,"* (Matthew 6:24).

Self-control and perseverance are the tools in the pruning process that bring about the fruit of true godliness. Purifying the heart comes about through the process of faith, goodness, knowledge, self-control, and perseverance.

141

The heart's cry is restoration in purity and holiness before our Father in heaven. In Hebrews 12:14 the writer says, *"Make every effort to live in peace with all men and to be holy; without holiness no one will see the Lord."* The doctrine of "holiness", or what is termed "the second blessing," was introduced into the church in 1888. The teaching was not a new thought, but a reintroduction to the church of the concept, *"Be holy as your Father in heaven in holy."* You cannot achieve godliness or god-likeness without holiness. The struggle we have with achieving holiness is we either give ourselves too much or too little grace in achieving and maintaining holiness. It is our heartfelt desire and commitment to be holy that our Lord honors. That does not mean we do not make mistakes, but we do not excuse away our mistakes through self-justification. Instead, we take full responsibility for our mistakes. Neither can we ignore or excuse away bad conduct, reasoning that it's okay because we do so many great things for God or we have such and such a position in the church.

The standard of holiness raised above us is the same as the one above our Father in heaven! We are our Father's children and our heart's desire is to be like him in heart and deed. Our heart's cry is to be as pure as he is pure and holy as he is holy. David said it so well in Psalm 24:3-4: *"Who may ascend into the hill of the Lord? Who may stand in His holy place? He who has clean hands and a pure heart."* Humility is the key to achieving and maintaining godliness.

Because of our godliness, we do not respond as our old-nature as previously dictated, but we take on a new nature, which bears the image of our Father in heaven. What does this new image look like? An image ruled by humility and purity of motives.

When we accepted Jesus as our Lord and Savior we were immediately clothed in new garments that define us as citizens of the kingdom of God. These new clothes represent our new nature, which contains the goodness of God.

God's goodness changes how we perceived this new reality. Our eyes begin to see things differently and our mind begins to reason differently. We process all this through his goodness.

The beauty of this is that we begin to take on the image of the one we love. Love has transformed us from the inside out, letting the King of Kings and Lord of Lords has his rightful place on the throne of our hearts. When the King of Kings is on the throne, we see the fullness of the kingdom of God established within.

Years ago, I struggled to overcome a memory of a very painful event that had happened in my life. I went through hours of forgiving anyone that may have knowingly or unknowingly been a part of what happened. No matter what I tried, I just could not get over it and felt doomed to replaying the event in my mind for the rest of my life.

These episodes were so devastating to my emotions that it would take me days to get back to a normal state. I began to take long walks to try to break out of the doldrums once these thoughts came flooding back into my mind. In my mind I would line up everyone in my life that had ever wronged me or I had wronged and spoke forgiveness and blessing over them as I passed them by on my walk.

A few years back, I read that the unconscious mind is unable to distinguish readily between what is vividly imagined and what we are really experiencing. If you are reliving a particular painful memory, the mind reacts by releasing dangerous levels of adrenaline, taking as long as 72 hours to come back to normal. So these walks I took were my way of getting out of the rut that was becoming deeper and deeper every time I would replay the memory.

A few years later as I was sitting on the porch of our home in Montana, I remembered the walks I took down the country road and how I would line up the people in my mind and, as I walked past them, I would forgive and bless them. Suddenly, I wondered what it was that I was trying to forget! What possibly had me in such a quandary? I began to search my memory for what it was that I had so desperately been trying to forget. I began to laugh as I realized that I was struggling to remember something that years ago I had so desperately tried to forget. So I stopped my search right there and thanked God for the victory that had occurred in my life. I was free from whatever it was that had plagued me for many years.

It reminded me of a cartoon. The cartoon showed a view of an old country road that had ruts in it that were very deep. The caption under the cartoon said, "Choose your rut carefully for you will be in it for the next 50 miles." From experience, I have found that the only way out of a rut is to jerk the wheel hard to the side and force yourself out of the rut. During my life, if I found myself in a deep rut of reliving an emotional crisis that had happened years previously, I did something drastic to get my mind from dwelling on the subject. It is true that the more you dwell on a particular difficult time, the deeper the rut becomes. That is why the walks were so important to me--they gave me a way to get out of the rut I was in and focus on something other than the pain I felt. I have found it is not so much the circumstances of life that shape us, such as a divorce, rape, job loss, death of a love one-- although these are very traumatic events in one's life. King-self likes to use these events to further ensure its own reign and rule over our life. That is why we must persevere until we see the change--and that change produces godliness.

I want to share something I learned in those walks. I never walked alone. Jesus was always with me during those times. I didn't realize it at the time, but later I could see how Jesus enabled me to not only forgive others but myself also. Galatians 5:16 says, *"So I say, live by the Spirit, and you will not gratify the desires of the sinful nature."* Some of my greatest victories happened from the things I learned on those long walks of forgiveness.

The old King will tell you that you are innocent, that no one understands you, and that your motives for doing something or reacting in the manner in which you did were well intentioned. We may have been hurt unfairly and we may have wronged another person--most likely a combination of both. By forgiving others and being accountable for our own negative behavior, we are able to keep a positive attitude in the midst of life's difficult situations. This is more important than we will ever realize. If we do not keep a pure heart and clean hands, we have lost the battle and the negative forces of sin can overtake us. No one wants to be a needless causality of war or live a life that is ineffective and unproductive.

Godliness is that place of profound change in which you find the character of Christ manifested in your life.

CHAPTER 16

BROTHERLY KINDNESS

Loving Your Neighbor

We must be consistent in our practice of self-control and perseverance. Peter warns us in 1 Peter 2:11, *"I urge you, as aliens and strangers in the world, to abstain from sinful desires, which war against your soul."* We are aliens and strangers living in a foreign land and we must be diligent not to succumb to the temptations that surround us each day. Until the new heaven and new earth appear, I can see no way to ever reach the place in our lives in which we can say we have arrived unless we remain alert. One look at how King David behaved at the pinnacle of his career should be enough for anyone of us. When David had reached his place of destiny, he began to rest on his achievements and committed his greatest sins.

Persevering into godliness is almost inconceivable to most of us. To be honest with you, I don't know many people who have arrived at this place in their lives. The people I have known who have made it to this stage in their lives I found to be the most clear minded, self-controlled, and humble people that I have ever met. People who live in a continual state of godliness seem to commune with God moment by moment in prayer.

Our persevering to godliness and brotherly kindness bring us to fulfill the Great Commandment found in Matthew 22:33-39: *"Love the Lord your God with all our heart and with all your soul and with all your mind. 'This is the first and greatest commandment.' And the second is like it: 'Love your neighbor as yourself.'"*

I have found that most people don't really like themselves; if they did, they would treat others better. It is true that many people want you to do better, just not better than themselves. I believe the reason this is true is that most people really do not like themselves. Brotherly kindness offers hospitality to others without grumbling. Brotherly kindness uses God's gifts to serve others and is faithful in administering God's grace in all its various forms. (See1 Peter 4:9-10). Without this commandment set in our hearts, how could we ever really have true compassion for all of humanity?

The more we experience God's love, the more we will love our brothers and sisters around us. Real affection for people and their situations will overwhelm us, in a good way, because His goodness and love rule our life. No more will we be superficial to the needs and feelings of others. We will not only care for others, but others will see Christ in us and know that we really do care for them. In fact, we will love others differently because we actually like ourselves. We like it when the King of Kings is on the throne. We can love much because we have overcome life's trials by the love of Christ in us.

When a Jewish man greets you with the word, "Shalom," he is wishing you peace. The deepest meaning of the word *shalom* is, "God's highest good to you." Peace is of no benefit if it is separate from Holiness. This is why every "peace agreement" that mankind puts together cannot work because it is always birthed through unrighteous motives. Hebrews 12:14 says, *"Make every effort to live in peace with all men and to be holy; without holiness no one will see the Lord."*

"Blessed are the peacemakers, for they shall be called sons of God," (Matthew 5:9). It would seem like every time we pick up a newspaper or turn on the news someone, somewhere is trying to broker a peaceful solution to an international situation. Trying to find peace is as difficult for individuals as it is for nations. Peace has come to be a very illusive commodity on earth.

Sin and Satan have affected the hearts of men and have led to a world without peace. Both Satan and sinful man have engaged God in a battle over who is sovereign. Who's the boss? Who's king? "Is it I?" or "Is it God?" "I fear it is I!" When King-self is first, peace is lost!

"The whole earth groans as in childbirth for the sons and daughters of God to be revealed." Peacemakers are those entrusted with restoring peace to individuals and nations. It would be impossible for any historian to find any era in the history of this world in which there has been true peace. Wars, both between individuals and nations, began when man fell in the garden. Our desire to be gods puts each person at odds with everyone else. There cannot be two gods, one must submit.

Our desire to be a "god" had disastrous consequences for all of creation. Creation was given to us to rule and have dominion over; when we gave that dominion over to Satan it caused creation to be subject to decay and death. It is important that we understand that creation is not comprised of inanimate objects that are void of life. When Jesus rode triumphantly into Jerusalem on the back of the donkey, he said, *"I tell you . . . if they keep quiet the stones will cry out,"* (Luke 19:40).

Creation is not a silent witness to the return of the sons and daughters of God. "The creation waits in eager expectation for the sons of God to revealed. For the creation was subjected to frustration, not by its own choice, but by the will of the one who subjected it, in hope that the creation itself will be liberated from its bondage to decay and brought into the glorious freedom of the children of God. *We know that the whole creation has been groaning as in the pains of childbirth right up to the present time," (Romans 8:19-22).*

Brotherly love is confrontational! It is one of its most important characteristics and one that people fail to understand because, it seems to be a contradiction to its very nature. Brotherly love will never succumb to allowing a person to live a lie for the sake of personal comfort. At its heart is a culture that honors the individual to such an extent that it speaks the truth in love, lifting a person into a higher plane rather than succumbing to lowering themselves into the pit. Jesus showed us all how to "love the Lord our God with all our hearts, soul and mind and to love our neighbors as ourselves." How can you love your neighbor if you will not tell him that he is facing eternal separation from God?

Jesus was not contradicting Hebrews 12:14 when he said in Matthew 10:34, *"Do not suppose that I have come to bring peace to the earth. I did not come to bring peace, but a sword. For I have come to turn a man against his father, a daughter against her mother, a daughter-in-law against her mother-in-law--a man's enemies will be the members of his own household."* What kind of peace is Jesus talking about? It is peace at any cost! Not peace for the sake of peace but peace that is brought through holding high the values of truth and righteousness. It's not that Christians love conflict, but that they love truth more. A true Christian will not forfeit truth and righteousness in exchange for his or her own comfort.

Truth has always been a two edged sword that both cuts and

heals. Anger and resentment must be removed from your life before truth and righteousness can heal the heart of man. The Christian who possesses brotherly love knows that the consequences of sin have blinded the eyes of man. Only truth can remove the blinders that hinder peace from entering in.

Who are these that show such brotherly kindness? James 3:18 says that *"Peacemakers who sow in peace raise a harvest of righteousness." "The wisdom that comes from heaven is first of all pure; then peace-loving, considerate, submissive, full of mercy and good fruit, impartial and sincere,"* (James 3:17). These are the true sons and daughters of love.

Brotherly kindness brings about conflict resolution. Conflict resolution is at the heart of true discipleship. It is the one quality of character we must possess if we are to confront those who are double minded in a godly manner. I know how difficult it is for many of us to confront someone. I remember many times when our children were smaller that I would have to punish them for something they had done or were in the process of doing. On one occasion, I pleaded with them asking them to please stop because the last thing I wanted to do was come out of the comfortable place I was in and go over and punish them.

When you are in a place of peace, the last thing you want is go into a place or situation that is confrontational. We are hesitant in going because our experiences have shown us that we

152

will certainly lose our peace. If the "old" is dominant over our "new" nature, we will find ourselves drawn to that which we are most like.

Yet Jesus is saying that when you take that very peace with you into the place of confrontation, the love you have for the person will transform the situation. Rather than allowing ourselves to be overwhelmed by the situation we overwhelm the situation by the love of Christ that is within us.

If we are not willing to interrupt and correct, how can we really exhibit brotherly love? If we do not in love point out God's truth and righteousness, we only settle on a peace which is a disappointing truce. Settling on peace for "peace's sake" compromises God's word and takes the person further from the heart of God. <u>Peace that costs us nothing will often cost the other person everything.</u>

Listen to what Jesus teaches about loving those who hate you. *"You have heard that it has been said, 'You must love your neighbor and hate those who hate you.' But I tell you, love those who hate you. Pray for those who do bad things to you and who make it hard for you. Then you may be the sons of your Father Who is in heaven,"* (Matthew 5:43-48).

Jesus gives us a very powerful picture of two instances of brotherly love in Matthew 5:38-42. *"You have heard that it was said, 'Eye for eye, and tooth for tooth.' But I tell you, Do not resist an evil person. If someone strikes you on the right cheek, turn to him the other also. And if someone wants to sue you and take your tunic, let him have your cloak as well. If someone forces you to go one mile go with him two miles. Give to the one who asks you, and do not turn away from the one who wants to borrow from you."*

The Law demands that the punishment must fit the crime. An eye for an eye and a tooth for a tooth is the law of our justice system. (See Exodus 21:23-24). It may restrain the deed but does little to restrain the person. Law touches the surface while love touches the center; one demands retribution while the other demands redemption. One is governed by its legal attitudes the other by its love attitudes. Loving your friends only is a product of the law of retribution; loving your enemies becomes the love that redeems those who are separated from you.

In Matthew 5:17 Jesus said this about the commandments in the Old Testament: *"Do not think I have come to abolish the Law or the Prophets; I have not come to abolish them but to fulfill them."* The commandments were a code of righteous behavior but Jesus came and gave it life, raising goodness out of a set of moral laws and requirements based on love. The difference is that one was devoted to an idea, the law, and produced the perfect Pharisee. And the second was devoted to an ideal, grace, and produced the perfect 'Lover'. Righteousness had as its goal a required duty while love has as its goal the abundant life. (John 10:10)

In brotherly love, you are open to the assumption that within every man are two men. One that is evil, whom you are not to resist, at least on his level and with his weapons, and another man, who is not evil, but who is susceptible to the appeal of love. Get to that man and you win, said Jesus. Retaliation always loses, even when it seems to win.

If I should strike you on the cheek, it is all about what I think of me, versus what I think of you. If I strike you on the cheek, you can rise to your feet in brotherly love and search to find within me a man who is susceptible to the appeal of love. You decide I'm worth it. So you offer the other cheek. And if I strike your other cheek it is now all about what you are really like versus what I am really like. The law of love takes you from resisting on his level and with his weapons and puts you on a much higher level. The law of love forces the man to go further than he is ready to go thus revealing his true character. His desire is to break your face, and you, as a Christian, try to break his heart.

When you choose to turn the other cheek, you move into a position where you are redefining the conflict and in doing so you assume moral control of the situation. This enables you to choose your own weapons and place of battle. You take the situation from out of his control and you compel him to stand on ground that he is not familiar with and to use weapons in which he has no skill.

"The weapons we fight with are not the weapons of the world. On the contrary, they have divine power to demolish strongholds. We demolish arguments and every pretension that sets itself up against the knowledge of God, and we take captive every thought to make it obedient to Christ," (2 Corinthians 10:4-6).

Jesus illustrated the force of brotherly kindness by using a real life situation, one that was familiar to many Jews at the time. The Romans had passed a law in which it was permissible for a Roman citizen to force a Jew to carry his load for one mile. There was not a Jewish person present who did not know of this law. It was humiliating in that it forced them into slavery and treated them like a beast of burden.

Listen carefully to what Jesus is saying. You know that if someone forces you to go one mile, you are his slave. You are required to obey and oftentimes we carry that burden begrudgingly.

But what if you decide to carry that burden an extra mile? Doesn't the situation dramatically change? The first mile made you a slave, but the second mile gives back your dignity. More importantly, it gives you moral control of the situation.

What's amazing is that this journey of love will change your position on the path. For the first mile, you walk behind the Roman as a slave. For the second mile, you walk beside the Roman as a friend, carrying his burden. For the first mile, you are in chains. For the second, you are free. Why? Because you decided to love. What's more, the Roman who thought he was better than you, now looks at you differently. He wonders who you are because you walk with such authority. His desire was to break your spirit, but with love you have broken through to his heart.

God's love is always at the center of brotherly kindness. Brotherly kindness will always speak the truth in love in order to save the other person from lies, pain, and sorrow. Confrontational love is one of the most powerful forces we have as a church. Confrontational love cuts through all pretenses and goes to the heart, revealing the answers that people so desperately seek.

CHAPTER 17

LOVE

Laid Down Lovers

In our pursuit of a lifestyle of self-control and perseverance, we are continually in the process of putting to death many of the deeds of our old nature. We now find ourselves consistent in our walk with God. When we find ourselves consistently walking in the state of godliness and brotherly love, we will be fulfilling the Great Commandment found in Matthew 22:37-39. Now the eighth and final signpost in our journey is love—and love is attainable. When we reach this last signpost, we are finally capable of God's love standard—which means that we can now go into all the world and make disciples. We are not only capable of making disciples that look like Jesus, but we enjoy fulfilling the Great Commission. (See Matthew 28:19).

For close to fifteen years I have known Rolland and Heidi Baker. For years I listened to Heidi's message, a call to all Christians to become "laid down lovers" of God. It was a call for us to die to the desires of the flesh and become "laid down lovers". At the end of her message, Heidi often ends up on the floor and says into the microphone, "Why don't you just give up and die?"

I know that dying to self is what I needed to do and the call to die daily is one that I believe in. The only trouble is that I have found that "dying daily" may as well be called "graduate level dying". I needed something that was more bite size. I searched for a long time and found a watch that had an alarm that would sound two beeps every hour. I needed this to remind myself to let God rule in my life and not my old nature. My goal was to die daily, but in truth I kept forgetting I was dead. I had all the good intentions of staying dead, I just forgot that I was dead. This watch reminded me that I was not God and kept me in that place of dependency before him. I needed a shorter leash to help keep me in line and help me be a true "laid down lover" of God, twenty-four hours a day, seven days a week.

When we consistently live in godliness and brotherly love, we enter into that place of being a laid down lover of God who is capable of producing disciples that look like Jesus.

Earlier, we defined a disciple as one who undertakes the disciplined instruction from another individual, with the sole intent that they adhere to the teachings of that person and take on their characteristics and life patterns. To take on the life patterns of Jesus and disciple others is a high and noble calling. Now we have reached that place in our lives where we are lovers of God, his disciples. Jesus looks at us and says, "Therefore go and make disciples of all nations, baptizing them in the name of the Father and of the Son and of the Holy Spirit, and teaching them to obey everything I have commanded you. And surely I am with you always, to the very end of the age," (Matthew 28:19-20).

What a commission! It's an honor and an awesome responsibility to disciple those who have given their hearts to Jesus.

A blessed man is one who remembers that nothing good can come from his old nature. This man remains in a constant state of emptiness before the Lord and fills his "self" with God's goodness and love each day. A man who has made it to the eighth signpost of love will bring his will into alignment with the will of his Father in Heaven. He is not self-confident, but is aware of his own inability and knows that apart from God he is incapable of attaining righteousness.

To reach that place of being an ambassador of the heart message of God, one must not be self-serving but self-sacrificing. He must love, no matter the cost to his personal comfort, and bring others into that place of being a heartfelt follower of Jesus.

One only has to read the book of First John to find someone who is passionate about love. John is the apostle of love. John admonishes us to love as God loves for he is love. 1 John 4:16 says, "God is love. Whoever lives in love lives in God, and God in him."

There are personal costs that are associated with every area that we have attained in our walk with God. There is a personal and corporate persecution that will arise from our being ambassadors of God, because this God-love puts us in direct opposition to the values of this world. Love is confrontational. Love confronts evil by its very presence and represents a value system that is contrary to any system the world has to offer. All worldly value systems are based on the King-self's desire to be equal or superior to God. Isaiah 64:6 says it well. "All our righteous acts are like filthy rags."

As followers of Jesus, we will have the same self-sacrificing attitude as our Master. To walk with Jesus is to make no apologies for being bold and courageous in the face of life's most difficult tasks. Without fear and shame we say, "I have denied my own self-interest with all of its self-pleasing attitudes. I will say and do whatever the Master has for me, no matter the cost."

This courageous, self-sacrificing lifestyle leads to the culmination of all that Peter is talking about. Peter's life points to love. You become a love ambassador for God. While everyone else hurries about their day, you carry a paternal fondness that is full of divine love for everyone you meet. Paternal love consumes you until you no longer try to elevate yourself because you are rooted and grounded in God.

Peter tells us that if we follow the pathway of Christian growth we will make our calling and election sure and we will not fall. He also says, "For if you possess these qualities in increasing measure, they will keep you from being ineffective and unproductive in your knowledge of our Lord Jesus Christ."

Peter was an ordinary man whose destiny was anything but ordinary. Jesus told his disciples in Matthew 16:24, *"If any man will come after me, let him deny himself, and take up his cross and follow me."* As awesome as Peter was in the gospels, it pales in comparison to the Peter we find in the epistles. Peter had to spend his time in his own garden of Gethsemane, and carry his own cross to a place called Golgotha.

That is what Peter wanted us to know. It is a simple teaching on the basics of our Christian walk. If we get caught up in our calling and election and forget that we are actually on a journey to our destiny, we risk being unproductive and ineffective. Remember what it says in the book of Revelation when he says to the church, "To those who overcome." He is not talking to the unsaved but to the church. We are called to be people who overcome the kingdom of this world and we do so by first denying ourselves. Then we pick up our cross and follow Jesus. Each one of us has a unique destiny that has been selected by

God for our lives. These destinies are as varied as the people who carry them. Whether you are an engineer, schoolteacher, carpenter, lawyer, cowboy or Indian chief you have a God ordained destiny to fulfill. Regardless of your earthly occupation, you are to make disciples and live out a message of love and hope to give to those whom God has placed around you. You are uniquely and wonderfully made, and equipped to meet the needs of a fallen world and the people you disciple will disciple others throughout time.

CHAPTER 18

THE WAY OF DISCIPLESHIP

Peter heard the call, responded, and became a follower of Jesus. During those first three years he was a loyal disciple, fully committed to Jesus. He would have been a pillar in any church he attended. But how much was still lacking within Peter? How much of the self-life still ruled Peter? After his fall we see a different Peter. Gone was the bravado and we are left with a humble man more interested in the things of God than the things of man. Did that mean he never made any more mistakes? I think we all know that is not true. He made mistakes and once was corrected in public by Paul, but he did not try to defend his actions by self-justifying what he had done. I believe Peter found that when his will was separate from the will of the Father, he was in a very dangerous place.

I do not know what has happened in your life. It would be foolish for me to think I could possibly understand all you have gone through. I wish I could tell you how many times I have wanted those who had done things to me to realize their mistake and with weeping come crawling over to me to ask forgiveness and clean my feet with their tears. The truth of the matter is, they probably do not even remember what they did and some may not even care. I guess I am waiting in vain for my fantasy to come true. So I have learned to shake the dust off my feet and go on. The only thing holding me in my cell is my own self-justification and pride--and they make very poor cellmates.

It is true that when you go through devastating situations that things will never turn out the same as you once thought they would. Once you get caught up in the battle, it is impossible to go back and start over like nothing ever happened. Life may not turn out like you had originally thought, but with the right attitude it will be still more than you ever dreamed. Let's read what our Father is telling us through the prophet Isaiah. Let's see what we can still accomplish with the life we now have. Isaiah 58:12, "*You'll use the old rubble of past lives to build anew, rebuild the foundations from out of your past. You'll be known as those who can fix anything, restore old ruins, rebuild and renovate, make the community livable again,*" (Isaiah 58:12, The Message).

Like David, we can still come out of our cave and take the journey to our destiny. It is important that we understand this one key thing--the circumstances that have happened to us, whether good or bad, fair or unfair, are all a part of the *call* and *election* that each one of us have to go through on our journey to our destiny. God did leave us signposts along the way.

166

On our journey from call to election we have to be careful not to lose sight of God's original plan and purpose for our lives. One of the primary ways this happens is when we allow another's destiny to take precedence over our own personal destiny. On our journey we will find ourselves walking alongside of many different individuals and groups of people. Each will have their own personal destinies to fulfill. God has brought us together for a season and when it comes time for us to go our separate ways we will both be stronger because of our time spent together. If we allow their destiny to override ours then when the time comes to part we may lose sight of who we were destined to become and until our memory returns we will find ourselves wandering aimlessly through life thinking that we have somehow failed. It is a good thing to be faithful and work hard helping another fulfill their calling, just be careful that you do not lose sight of your calling, election and destiny in the process. Your life is important to God and your destiny will impact eternity.

The pursuit of our destiny will cost us everything. King David wanted to build an altar to the Lord on the threshing floor that belonged to Araunah the Jebusite. Araunah wanted to give the land to David free of charge, but David said to him, *"No, I insist on paying you for it. I will not sacrifice to the Lord my God burnt offerings that cost me nothing,"* (2 Samuel 24:24. The journey from self-control to perseverance to godliness and finally love will cost you everything. *"For whoever wants to save their life will lose it, but whoever loses their life for me and for the gospel will save it,"* (Mark 8:35).

Today we are in a battle and there are wounded people all around us. The enemy does not want us to live through it and survive. Satan would like to see us either surrender and become totally under his control or, if we do give our hearts to Jesus, he wants our lives to be miserable. The battle is real and our enemy is like a roaring lion looking for someone to devour.

Satan asked to sift Peter like wheat but Jesus prayed that his faith would not fail. It is no different today. Satan is asking to sift your neighbor, wife, children and you like wheat. When Jesus looked at Peter that day by the shore, he did not accuse him of anything. He just asked, "Peter do you love me?" There may have been a time in your life where the circumstances were so overwhelming and like Peter you felt the whole world had come crashing down on your head. You relive every detail of what you said, he said, they said until you are sick of it. The *what-ifs* have made such a deep rut in your mind and emotions that the best thing you have to hope for is to mask the pain--anything so that you don't have to live with the disappointments the memory brings every time it stirs within you.

The simple truth is that Jesus knows what really happened and in the midst of it all he is looking at you right now like he did Peter so long ago and is asking, "Do you love me?" Simple words, but it is really the only thing that matters. When we see ourselves reacting from our old nature, we have no excuses left to justify our actions and the only thing we can do is reply, "Jesus, I love you." Then we will experience the freedom to walk out of our cell into the light of our destiny, pick up our cross, and follow Jesus.

When Peter said, "Jesus, I love you", Jesus reminded him of his destiny. (John 21:18-19) He looked into Peter's eyes and said, "Follow me." Once we have told Jesus we love him, once we have laid the world at his feet, then we are ready to follow him to the end. Now that you are a follower of Jesus he says this to you, *"And when you have turned back, strengthen your brothers."* This is the journey to our destiny, and we will leave no one behind.

ABOUT THE AUTHOR

Rex Burgher is an author and international conference speaker. Rex has a passion to see people's lives transformed into the image of God.

Rex and his wife, Lois, have been happily married for 36 years. They have two daughters and six grandchildren.

In 2001, Rex and Lois co-founded Kingdom Life Ministry in Dillsburg, Pennsylvania. Together they have ministered in over 16 nations around the world. Their story reverberates in the hearts of all those who desire to be used by God. Their lives speak of one's who dared to step out of their comfort zone and say, "yes" to God.

Rex has authored two books, 'Journey to your Kingdom Destiny' and 'Our Father's Heartbeat'.

For more information, visit www.klifemin.org

 Blogginginthekingdom.blogspot.com

 Kingdom Life Ministry, Rex & Lois Burgher

Books by Rex Burgher

'Our Father's Heartbeat'
&
'Journey to your Kingdom Destiny'

Publications of:

KINGDOM LIFE MINISTRY

To Order Additional Books:
On Line, By Phone or by Mail:

On-line
www.klifemin.org

Phone:
717-502-0343

Mail:
Kingdom Life Ministries
PO Box 583
Dillsburg, PA 17019, USA
(include a check for $15.99 + $3.00 for shipping and handling)

40% Discounts will be given to purchases of **5** or more books:
Phone: 717-502-0343
Email: info@klifemin.org